What I saw at Bethesda

by

CHARLES SHERIDAN JONES

With an Introduction by

J. Elwyn Hughes

First Impression – 2003

ISBN 1 84323 324 X

© J. Elwyn Hughes 2003

J. Elwyn Hughes has asserted his right under the Copyright, Designs and Patents Act, 1988, to be identified as Author of this Work.

What I saw at Bethesda by Charles Sheridan Jones was first published in 1903 by Brimley Johnson, London, W.C.

New Edition with Introduction by J. Elwyn Hughes November 2003

Printed in Wales at
Gomer Press, Llandysul, Ceredigion

CONTENTS

ACKNOWLEDGEMENTS

My very sincere gratitude is due to Mary Barnett, of London, daughter of Charles Sheridan Jones, for her invaluable support and co-operation over the years in our quest for more information about her father. She has never seen a copy of *What I saw at Bethesda* and I should like to dedicate this present publication to her in memory of her father.

Mary's husband, Barney, helped as much as he possibly could, and their son, Nicholas, was also able to send me some relevant material.

I also wish to thank Eryl Wyn Rowlands, Llangefni, for succeeding in finding me an original copy of *What I saw at Bethesda* – a publication that must be one of the most important acquisitions in my collection of Bethesda local history material.

My very good friend and former colleague, Dennis Evans, Bangor, cast his critical eye over my Introduction and I gratefully acknowledge his assistance and expertise.

I am indebted to Gomer Press for accepting my suggestion to reprint *What I saw at Bethesda* and, in particular, to Ceri Wyn Jones, English Publications Editor at Gomer, for his support and valuable guidance throughout the process of preparing this work for publication.

J. Elwyn Hughes
November, 2003

INTRODUCTION

by J. Elwyn Hughes

Our story is about a young Londoner who ventured into a seething cauldron of industrial oppression and discontent and emerged as prime witness to a drama of extreme hardship and suffering. His testimony of what he saw a century ago – long lost and forgotten over the years – is retrieved and revived exactly one hundred years later. We may now judge for ourselves why he addressed his dedication to 'the women who suffered in silence, the old men who died in exile, the children who starved at home' and to 'Bethesda's dead'. Our story must, therefore, begin at Bethesda.

BETHESDA

Bethesda, a Hebrew word meaning 'a house of mercy', was the name adopted by a group of Welsh Independent Nonconformists in North Wales for the chapel they built on the side of the new London-Holyhead A5 road in 1820. Within a couple of years of the chapel being built, when other buildings began to spring up around the new road, Bethesda was adopted as the name of the fast-growing and flourishing village – 'almost deserving the name of town', as one early visitor put it.

Thomas Telford's new road ran through the Nant Ffrancon Pass and the Ogwen Valley, almost parallel with the River Ogwen, through an area that boasts of 'some of the most beautiful scenery in the world', as one traveller wrote towards the end of the nineteenth century (after condemning Bethesda's High Street as 'the most furiously ugly row of houses that roof was ever put to'). Approaching Bethesda from the south, one encounters a breathtaking view of some of the highest mountains in Wales, with Tryfan, just over 3000 feet, steep and craggy, being the mountain chosen by John Hunt and Edmund Hillary for practice and preparation for the ascent, and eventual conquest, of Everest in the early 1950s. Within a stone's throw of this rockiest mountain in Wales, we have the highest home in Wales, the smallest chapel in Wales, and Llyn Ogwen, reputed to be the shallowest lake in Wales.

Further down the valley, we see the gigantic slate tips of the Penrhyn Slate Quarry that used to be, and probably still is, the largest slate quarry in the world.

THE JAMAICA CONNECTION

The story of Bethesda itself, however, really begins in 1781 and has its roots, strangely enough, in the Caribbean. That year an Englishman, named John Pennant, died in Jamaica, leaving all his wealth, amassed from his vast sugar plantations (where he had £75,000 worth of slaves), to his son, Richard. After marrying Anne Susannah (of Llandygái, between Bethesda and Bangor), heiress of the Penrhyn Estate, in 1765, Richard Pennant conducted a survey of the estate. He found 80 men working on the mountain slopes, using very primitive methods of quarrying slates for their own use. He realised the tremendous potential of this natural mineral wealth and when his father died and left him a vast fortune, he immediately began spending his inheritance on developing what was soon to become the biggest slate-quarrying operation in the world. Between 1784 (when his men started excavating the big hole in the side of the Fronllwyd mountain) and 1801, Richard Pennant, created Baron Penrhyn of County Louth in 1783, had spent approximately £120,000, not only on developing the quarry itself, but also on building a road and a six-mile narrow-gauge railroad from the quarry to his newly-developed harbour at Bangor. This railway was one of the earliest railroads in Britain.

Baron, or Lord, Penrhyn died in 1808 and was succeeded by a relative, George Hay Dawkins-Pennant who, in 1828, started building the pseudo-Norman-style Penrhyn Castle about three miles north of the quarry. Dawkins-Pennant died in 1841, shortly after his grand, if rather overpowering, castle was completed. He was followed by Edward Gordon Douglas-Pennant, the first Baron Penrhyn of Llandygái, who, in 1885, was succeeded by his son, George Sholto Douglas-Pennant, about whom his father said to his loyal quarrymen, 'Do not cross George, he will never forgive', a chilling threat that was to become stark reality between 1896 and 1903. Hugh Napier Douglas-Pennant, Fourth Baron Penrhyn, who died in 1949, was the last Lord Penrhyn to live at the Castle which is now owned by the National Trust, and attracts over 130,000 visitors each year.

EARLY SETTLERS

Towards the end of the first decade of the eighteenth century, it is estimated that the quarry was making an annual profit of some £7000 and this figure increased every year, especially after the war between Britain and France ended in 1815, after which the slate industry developed rapidly. Many men, from all parts of North Wales, flocked into the area to work in the Penrhyn Quarry and, with a workforce of 1000 in 1819, over 24,000 tons of slate product, worth £58,000, left the quarry. At first, the men stayed in 'barracks' (where it is said that the fleas were as big as rats!) and returned to their homes every weekend until they could afford to build little cottages and rows of terraced houses for their families close to the ever-expanding new industry.

The development of the quarry, the increase in trade and export of slates, the steady rise in the number of employees, and the building of the A5 through the valley, all contributed to the birth of the new village – Bethesda – and a number of minor villages and hamlets, five of which, together with a church and a sizeable lake, are now buried under the quarry-waste tips. By 1845, there were almost 3000 men working at the quarry and about 15,000 people in the area were dependent on the slate industry.

LANGUAGE, RELIGION AND CULTURE

The people attracted into the area by the new industry came from places where the Welsh language was the mother tongue of almost all the inhabitants. In fact, almost everyone in Wales could speak Welsh during the nineteenth century. They naturally brought their language into the area, making quarrying a Welsh-speaking industry, with very few quarrymen, especially in those early years, able to speak any English at all. Whenever they needed to communicate with their masters – the successive Lords of Penrhyn, quarry and land owners, and their loyal agents, who could not speak Welsh – they had to do this in English either through an interpreter or in written translations from Welsh. No wonder the monoglot Welshman (and even the bilingual Welshman in more recent years) was deemed a second-class citizen in his own country.

The early quarry workers brought not only their language into the area but also the culture, customs and habits of their own different localities. Whereas the Church had a strong foothold in most areas, it soon had to compete in the Ogwen Valley (or Dyffryn Ogwen, as it is known even in English nowadays) with the fast-growing Nonconformist movement, which was introduced into the area towards the end of the eighteenth century. Soon, different denominations began building their chapels, the first 'proper' Calvinistic Methodist chapel being erected in 1816, followed in 1820 by the building of the first Independent Nonconformist Chapel, called 'Bethesda'. Other chapels followed and towards the end of the nineteenth century there were four or five Churches in the area and over 30 chapels.

Added to their passion in religious matters, the quarrymen's thirst for knowledge and their strong desire to better themselves by learning about various branches of culture were very prominent features in the social structure of Bethesda and district. Even in the quarry itself, every opportunity would be seized upon to discuss various topics of current affairs and during their lunch-breaks the quarrymen would hold quite formal discussions in their eating-sheds, under the guidance of an elected chairman, on different aspects of religion, education, literature, music, history, politics, local administration, industrial topics, etc. Different sections of the quarry would have not only their own football teams competing against each other but also their own singing groups and choirs. In the evenings, church and chapel meetings of different descriptions would be held regularly, and well-attended concerts, plays, debates, lectures, etc., were held very frequently in all areas within Dyffryn Ogwen.

ESCAPE!

And it was in their religion, their cultural activities, their meetings and debates, their simple pastimes, and in their homes and families, that the quarrymen found their escape, not only from their extremely hard work at the Quarry – every day of the year except Christmas Day, whatever the weather – but also from the almost inhuman way that they were often treated, from the intimidation they had to endure, and from the unfairness and injustice they had to suffer on a daily basis. When they were not at chapel, at Eisteddfodau or at meetings of various kinds, they would tend to their gardens or allotments, they would make improvements to their homes – that were more often than not under rent from the Penrhyn Estate – and some of them would spend their evenings supporting local victuallers. It must be added that inns and taverns were as numerous in the area as were chapels and churches! To supplement their earnings at the quarry, a few quarrymen were able to keep some poultry, a pig or a couple of sheep, perhaps, or even a cow or two.

One characteristic that permeated throughout Dyffryn Ogwen was that special brand of humour often found in areas where life is hard. Despite – or more probably because of – the hard and, at times, almost intolerable, working conditions, the quarrymen, their families and their friends were very quick to appreciate the funny side of life, and countless anecdotes, stories and jokes are related and remembered locally. But even a smile was difficult to raise when spirits were at their lowest, during troubled times at the Penrhyn Quarry.

DISPUTES AND STRIKES

Following two fairly minor disputes in 1825 and 1846, the first strike of real significance occurred at the Penrhyn Quarry in 1865. The men, dissatisfied with their lot, attempted to form a Union; Lord Penrhyn wouldn't hear of it and threatened to close not only his quarry but also his cottages (his men's homes which he claimed he owned). The men returned to work after a fortnight. Further strike action in 1874 – lasting about three months – ended in victory for the quarrymen and established the newly-formed North Wales Quarrymen's Union on a firm footing. After this show of determination, circumstances improved at the quarry and life was just that little bit better for the men. However, this was not to last, and matters worsened considerably from the mid-1880s onwards, after George Sholto Douglas-Pennant had taken over control of the Quarry from his father, Edward Gordon – for whom the quarrymen had some respect and even a hint of affection. Within a short time, while it became patently obvious that the men could not accept the new regime and its escalating oppression, it was just as clear that the management would not budge an inch in compromise or concession, apparently electing for confrontation rather than conciliation. After many years of debate and deliberation, talks and correspondence, the men could no longer stand the hardship, the poor working conditions, low pay, and many instances of favouritism at the quarry. They came out on strike in 1896 and stayed out for 11 months before finally having to concede to the power of Penrhyn. This strike had a crippling effect on the men and their families and life was very hard for all concerned. But this was only the beginning, since worse was to come at the turn of the century.

Y STREIC FAWR – THE GREAT STRIKE: 1900-1903

The sad state of affairs at the Penrhyn Quarry in the latter years of the nineteenth century led to one of the longest strikes in British Trade Union history. The men, on the one hand, could no longer stand the way they were being treated while, on the other hand, George Sholto Douglas-Pennant – Lord Penrhyn – was just as adamant that he would not surrender to his men's demands. This situation, which has been well documented in many publications (none better than *The North Wales Quarrymen, 1874-1922*, R. Merfyn Jones, Cardiff, 1981), dealt a severe blow not only to the men and their families but also to the slate industry at Penrhyn Quarry – and the problems and difficulties of these times were to have a long-term effect on Bethesda and the whole locality.

About six months after the strike broke out, some 500 men (out of an estimated total workforce of almost 3000) returned to work at the quarry, lured by the golden sovereign offered by Lord Penrhyn to all those who returned. He also had a row of houses built for the ones who were willing to return to work. These men, who did great harm to the strikers' cause, were branded as 'traitors' (the modern day *blacklegs* or *scabs*) but there was another side to this coin. Still reeling from the 1896-97 dispute, many of the men, while they were on strike, were forced to watch their wives and children having to go without even the bare essentials of life; many were on the point of starvation, and the option of going back to work and earning some money once again was a temptation that these men could not resist. Others, it must be added, decided that they, too, had to provide for their families and about 1500 men left the area, some never to return, for the coalfields of South Wales and other areas in Britain and overseas.

Obviously, the rift in the community led to all kinds of problems not only during the strike itself, when there were unavoidable confrontations between strikers and traitors – even within families and

and the descriptive and historical matter is written in a most racy style, no important feature of interest being overlooked'.

In 1917, CSJ published *London in War Time*, '. . . a most picturesque contribution to contemporary social history' according to *The Financial Times*, while *The Daily Mirror* (of Manchester, USA) wrote 'A most vivid presentation of the dwellers in the great city, of their fortitude and fearlessness, their courage, and of all the great and noble qualities which England has demonstrated since the war'. *President Wilson: the Man and his Message* appeared in 1918 – 'An arresting picture of the great man', according to one critic.

1920 saw the publication of two of his books: *Bolshevism – Its Cause and Cure*. 'A clear expression of the evils that lie behind this false and cruel system . . . I hope the book will have an immense distribution', said the Rt. Hon. Sir Gilbert Parker, while Coulson Kernahan judged it to be 'The soundest, sanest, and most illuminating work on Bolshevism which I have seen'. The second book was *A Short Life of Washington*, which *The Bookman* reckoned to be '. . . a worthy piece of work, happily carried out by Mr Jones to give a brief, swift narrative of Washington's life and career for English readers. . . . Mr Jones traces his history with admirable clearness, ease, and proportion. The book is very much to be commended both for scope and manner'. *The Call to Liberalism*, published in 1921, was said to be '. . . full of interesting and valuable information which everyone should know' and C. W. Darbishire, Independent Liberal Candidate for Westbury Division of Wiltshire, wrote to CSJ, prior to publication: 'I congratulate you on a masterly exposition of the true Liberal standpoint, and I hope, when you publish the book, you will see that it is placed in the hands of every Liberal Candidate, and the sooner the better'.

THE DEATH OF CHARLES SHERIDAN JONES

Unfortunately, no information has come to light about CSJ's latter years but we do know that he died from a cerebral haemorrhage at The Orchard, Ashdon, Essex, on January 24, 1925, aged 50. His sister, Ada, whose address is given as 3 Fleet Street, London, E.C.4. on the death certificate, was with him when he died and it was she who registered his death. Obituary notices appeared in *The Daily News*, *The Star*,

Evening News, and many other newspapers. The *Sheffield Daily Telegraph* of January 26, 1925, who surprisingly put his age as 90, described him as 'A keen trade unionist', but got it somewhat wrong when it added: 'he organised the Bethesda quarrymen in the Penrhyn strike'.

Although it has not been possible to find any real Welsh connection as far as Charles Sheridan Jones was concerned, a little anecdote about his widow may be of interest. During the Second World War blitz, Marion Sheridan Jones sold her house in London and went to stay with 'a kind woman' in Trawsfynydd, Wales. The sad twist in this story's tail is that Marion put her things in store, only for it to be discovered later that all her possessions had been rifled and most of Charles Sheridan Jones's books and papers were missing.

But *What I saw at Bethesda* has survived and in spite of its journalistic peculiarities, its flowery language and its dramatic touches of exaggeration and minor embellishments here and there, this reprinted edition will afford the reader an insight into what one outsider actually saw, and wrote about, at Bethesda during the *Streic Fawr*.

WHAT I SAW AT BETHESDA

BY

C. SHERIDAN JONES

SPECIAL CORRESPONDENT OF "THE DAILY NEWS"

LONDON
R. BRIMLEY JOHNSON
8, YORK BUILDINGS, ADELPHI, W.C.

The 28 year-old Charles Sheridan Jones as member of the W. J.
Parry Defence Fund Committee

To the Memory of

BETHESDA'S DEAD
THE WOMEN WHO HUNGERED IN SILENCE
THE OLD MEN WHO DIED IN EXILE
THE CHILDREN WHO STARVED AT HOME

I DEDICATE

THIS EFFORT TO DEPICT THEIR SUFFERINGS AND
MAKE CLEAR THE CAUSE

A view of the Penrhyn Slate Quarry, Bethesda

Looking from Pantdreiniog Co-operative Quarry over Bethesda Chapel and part of
the village towards the Penrhyn Slate Quarry

CHAPTER I

BETHESDA'S ORDEAL

BETHESDA still stands defiant. To one on the spot that fact is clear before all others. The quarrymen have been tried almost beyond endurance, but they are still unconquered. As I write, the sun is slowly rising from behind the snow-clad mountains, which form so splendid a background to this terrible industrial tragedy. In the High Street below one can see a stream of men and women on their way to the railway station. Some are sitting on carts, on which are piled high their household gods. They are leaving Bethesda for ever, and as the man takes in sullen silence his last look at the old home, among the delectable mountains, the woman rocks herself to and fro, and shuts her eyes, as though she dared not look. Others are leaving their wives and children behind them. They are working away from Bethesda, and they had come home to get a glimpse of their families. That glimpse is over now, and the station platform is lined by their wives, who stand with drawn faces and set lips. They say little; but, as the train steams out, the women try bravely to raise a cheer, a cheer that ends in sobs.

Saunter back from the station to Bethesda, and – you will find a singular spectacle indeed – that of a town once thriving and prosperous, now paralysed. The High Street is empty. Half the shops have their shutters up. In the doorways stand the tradesmen of the place, racking their brains for occupation. Ruin, complete and overwhelming, faces nearly every one of them. For two years the £12,000 that in happier days left the quarry as wages has ceased absolutely so far as Bethesda is concerned. The shops have now few customers. Fourteen hundred of the men are away. True, those working in the coalfields of South Wales – who have just ended their Christmas vacation – earn good wages, and manage to send home enough to keep the wolf from the door; but others, less fortunate, get but scant pay at the Rhydr water-dams, or in the quarries of Nantlle. They can barely

1

scrape together a few shillings every week for the wife and bairns they so seldom see. Seven hundred of the strikers have no employment at all. They and their families must contrive to live on the Union pay of ten shillings a week. Other families – those of widows, chiefly – have not even this wretched pittance. They look to the Relief Committee literally for the bread of life, and the committee gives them 3s 6d a week! Small wonder there is no industry in Bethesda, that the shopkeepers are ruined, that the whole place wears the air of a deserted town, once busy with the hum of life, but now stricken and listless, condemned to emptiness and idle days!

Yet, search Bethesda over, and you may not find one ragged figure. The people are curiously proud. In this, their darkest hour, they still contrive to keep spick and span. But, win a way into their homes, into the trim slate cottages set in neat rows along the hills to the right and left of the High Street, and dreadful scenes of suffering confront you. I call one to mind now. A distracted striker is trying to rock a fretful child to sleep. Upstairs his wife is lying sick nearly unto death, and the man is fearful lest the child's cries should break in on her sleep, the one chance of recovery the woman has. In the corner are the other children, hushed, and with the pallor of starvation on their faces. The man has no money, no aid, and only a little food in the house. He dare not leave the house to get help, and he has had no sleep for two nights!

That is no uncommon case at Bethesda. And for a good reason. Work in the coal-fields plays havoc with the men's lungs, accustomed to a rarefied atmosphere. At Rhydr water-dams all but the strongest get rheumatism. At Nantlle, in the open quarries, cold seizes them. Time and time again they come back weak and enfeebled to be nursed back to health only at the cost of their wife's. Then, when she is ill, the children are neglected, and fall sick also. In almost every home sickness runs this vicious circle.

And it is the children who suffer most. As I write, the words of the headmaster of the British school ring in my ears. Every other day, he tells me, some of his scholars are at his door begging bread. Others need boots, and cannot attend school. One sees them languidly trying to play on the tipping ground of Pantreniog, the Co-operative quarry, which Mr. W. J. Parry, that indomitable champion of the men, rescued from desuetude at the commencement of the present struggle. Everywhere childhood is changed at Bethesda. 'They have forgotten how to play,' one woman told me, speaking of her four children, whom I found in a cottage at Caellwyngrydd, on the point of sitting down to a supper of dry bread! That bread is the outward and visible sign of the relief now reaching Bethesda – relief that stands literally, between the people and absolute starvation. That relief needs to be enormously increased. True, the English Trade Unions have given nobly to the quarrymen. The choirs, made up from the quarrymen and their daughters, have won hundreds of pounds by their singing, which has caused a furore in the industrial cities of the north. The London Committee, by a series of extraordinary exertions, have raised £5500 for the men within an incredibly short space of time. But the fact stands that, as I write to-night, misery and privation are present in hundreds of the quarrymen's cottages. Children are going crying to bed unfed, women are sobbing that they cannot fill their mouths. The physical standard of the race is being broken.

And this mountain community is not being weakened by lack of food alone. Some of its best specimens are shaking the dust of the place off their feet for ever, and are seeking elsewhere the reasonable conditions denied them here. The race is being scattered to please one man.

Some of these departures have a poignant pathos. To-day a quarryman, who had reached eighty-three years of age, and through sixty of these had laboured for Lord Penrhyn, left to join his son in America. The old man had to take his last look at his wife's grave, and to turn his back for ever on his old home, on everything almost that he had cared for since childhood. It must have been a dreadful wrench, and the case does not stand alone. Young men have taken their last farewells of their mothers. Young wives have been parted from their husbands. Children have forgotten what their fathers are like. Everywhere one sees signs of exodus. The day following my arrival I attended worship in one of the numerous chapels this Puritan community sustains. It was a most curious, a pathetic spectacle. From the pulpit the pastor poured out his discourse in eloquent Cymric, but it was to empty pews he preached. Not more than half a dozen worshippers were present. His congregation had been driven by Penrhynism to the coalfields of South Wales, or further afield to the quarries of Newfoundland.

Those that remain are divided by a terrible bitterness. I can best bring home its force by describing an incident I witnessed to-day, trifling in itself, but very instructive as to the temper of the people. In a little side street in Bethesda I found the household goods of three families who were moving to Tregarth. The goods were standing in the road, no one could be got to move them. Their owners were 'bradyrs' (traitors), a little girl told me, and not a soul at Bethesda, it seemed, could be found to handle their belongings. Neither love nor money could procure the families the use of a cart, and for some hours the furniture remained in the roadway. Not long since two "bradyrs" entered a place of worship at Tregarth, and the extraordinary spectacle presented itself to the preacher of the whole congregation rising en masse, and leaving in dignified silence. In their eyes the holy place had been desecrated, and they could not suffer themselves to remain.

This bitterness between the two parties has some very curious results. The recent disorder at Bethesda has, I find, not merely been exaggerated, but woefully misrepresented. In large part it has been the work of the 'bradyrs' themselves, whose policy it is to irritate the strikers by wanton and unprovoked attacks. Some of the 'bradyrs' walk about of an evening flourishing revolvers. In one case, at Tregarth, they pursued and fired after a striker, who was not, however, hit. It is safe to assert that the police have had far more trouble from the 'bradyrs' than from the strikers. The leaders of the latter are constantly impressing on the rank and file the importance of good conduct. But the 'bradyrs' are defended by Lord Penrhyn's own solicitor when, as now frequently happens, they are prosecuted at Bangor, and they feel that they have behind them the prestige of the Penrhyn family, and that it was not for nothing their employer and his son addressed them recently in the quarry, and promised a continuance of support. For 'blacklegs' to assault strikers, and for the strikers to be credited with the offence, is something new in labour struggles. But the Bethesda dispute has witnessed even that crowning irony.

The police, as admitted by the recent report of the Committee of Enquiry appointed by the Carnarvonshire County Council, have been throughout arbitrary and biased. They have actively befriended the 'bradyrs.' They have positively persecuted the strikers by frivolous and manufactured charges which they have been unable to sustain. They have assaulted strikers, their wives and children, and have done more to provoke the patient, law-abiding quarrymen than even the 'bradyrs' themselves. I deal at length with this scandal later. First, let us enter some of the homes of the people.

4

Come to Caellwyngrydd, a suburb of Bethesda. Caellwyngrydd has for months past been a starving district. I question if anywhere else in the world can there be found a parallel for the spectacle it presents – that of a number of skilled workmen, temperate and thrifty to a degree, yet lacking, with their wives and children, the actual necessaries of life. It is impossible for me to describe the scenes that I witnessed to-day in the homes of these half-distracted people, and fortunately I need not do so. The facts are eloquent, and speak for themselves. I need only set out in skeleton form some of the more representative cases which I have selected from a mass of others.

Take first the case of Mrs. Richard Jones. Her house was, I found, absolutely bare, though scrupulously clean. When I and the Relief Committeemen arrived she was cutting some bread, that she herself had made, into slices. That bread was the only food she had in the house with which to stay her five children's hunger, and but for the Relief Committee (who had supplied the flour) she would have lacked even that. She had not a drop of milk. She was without so much as a lump of sugar. There was a little burnt treacle and some tea leaves, that had been used over and over again. This was all she could add to the brew to make the children's meal. Small wonder the little ones looked haggard and worn. They had known worse times: their mother told me that once, half demented, she had gone out and begged from door to door for food. She had to walk far before she could find anyone to give her more than pity. In this case the husband, a striker, has been unemployed for eighteen months. At the commencement of the present struggle he got work in the Lancashire collieries, but an accident compelled him to return home. He and his family have had nothing since to live upon except the Union allowance of 10s a week. Now, thanks to *The Daily News*, the Relief Committee will be able to add at least a trifle to this wretched sum. I found an even sadder case. At the next cottage we visited we were faced by a woman in the last extreme of suffering and misery. She herself was expecting very shortly to be confined. Her husband lay prostrate with rheumatism. She had literally nothing in the house with which to get food, and her husband's strike allowance of ten shillings a week from the Quarrymen's Union did not become due till next month. True, the husband has been unemployed only for a week or two, but his earnings (he worked at Rhyrdr) have not admitted of his sending more than ten shillings a week home, and his

5

wife has nothing to fall back upon now that she is ill, and her two children are clamouring for food. Small wonder, therefore, that she burst into tears when told that a grant had been made her from the Relief Committee! That grant, alas, was only six shillings, but to her it was priceless. Her children would be fed at last. My own feelings I do not chronicle. Indeed, if I allowed my mind to dwell upon the facts I could not state them at all.

One marvels as one visits cottage after cottage in this stricken district at the extraordinary dogged honesty of the people. Nearly all of them told me with a touch of pride that they had paid their rent – a matter of two shillings to half a crown a week – all through this dreadful time. Among all these sufferers I did not find one single waverer. The men all scouted the idea of returning to the quarry on Lord Penrhyn's 'terms' of unconditional surrender. The women answered even more fiercely. 'I would sooner die,' one told me, 'than that he should go in.'

On the hillside leading up to Moel Faban we met two women wretchedly clad. One was looking after some sheep; the other, Mrs. Morgan, the wife of an unemployed striker, has two children, and nothing but the strike allowance to feed them on. Her children were living practically on the potatoes that she raised in her garden. Another woman told me that she had supported herself for months by gathering cockles; and more than one confessed that but for the Relief Committee and occasional credit from tradespeople they must have succumbed. *The Daily News* and the London Committee have removed that danger, but the suffering that still remains is terrible.

Consider the case of Albert Rutglede. Before the strike he was gardener to a quarry official. His wife's brothers were strikers, and the official urged Rutglede to get them to submit, but the gardener preferred to mind his own business, and was accordingly discharged. To-day I found his wife in tears, sobbing her heart out over a child. Her husband does odd jobs in the district, and manages to bring home perhaps seven shillings a week. Frequently she told us she has been for a fortnight without coal. She has to pay six shillings a month for rent, and can barely keep body and soul together. Her house was a model of cleanliness.

That is what Bethesda's ordeal means to the women and children. Let me illustrate by a true, strange story the kind of sacrifices it involves on the part of the men. A striker went some eight months ago to South Wales, seeking work, with his two sons. After some time his daughter fell dangerously ill, and was recalled home. Then his son got bad, and had to come home also. They were seven in family, and when week after week went by, and neither father nor son got work, they were hard put to it to live. Presently there came an ejectment notice from Mr. Trench, Lord Penrhyn's estate agent; the man was behind with his rent. He applied to the Relief Committee, who staved off the danger of ejectment by paying half the rent. They also got the man work at Penmaenmawr, and paid his fare there. Thither he went, but not to remain.

His family were by this time in dire straits, and the man could send them but little. There is no doubt that their condition preyed on his mind. He returned and went into the quarry, and became mad within six weeks.

The explanation is simple. The man had been fervent in his belief in the justice of the cause, and keen in his denunciation of the 'bradyrs.' When hunger drove him into the quarry his remorse was dreadful. Those who witnessed his distress, and heard his frenzied self-accusations, still speak with awe of him. He felt as another Judas, and went weeping to the men's leaders for consolation and forgiveness. Finally, in an excess of despondency, the poor wretch hanged himself!

This man, no doubt, was hyper-emotional and hysterical, a weak brother. But it is impossible to escape the moral of his case. Funds did not permit of his having more effective assistance, and lack of funds is the key to the situation. Just as it drove this poor wretch to moral destruction and to suicide so, if it be not speedily met, it may drive stronger men to surrender.

This, then, is Bethesda's ordeal. She has endured it now for two years and three months. And I shall show that, fearful as that ordeal is, it is to avoid a worse fate that she still endures. Her surrender would mean what, at all costs, must be averted – the destruction of a fine and gifted race, struggling for dear life against one man; a man whose motto, carved in stone on his castle gate, looks down on the ruined countryside: 'Aequo Animo' – with an even mind!

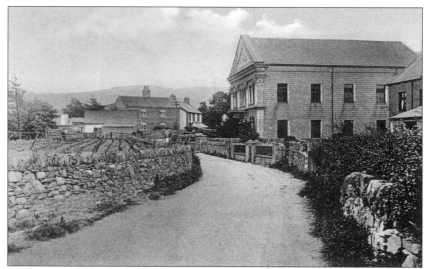

Shiloh Chapel, Tregarth (Wesleyan Methodist), where the whole congregation stood up one Sunday evening during the three-year strike and quietly walked out of the Chapel when two 'traitors' walked in

Tanrhiw Road, Tregarth. A row of houses built by Lord Penrhyn for the men who had returned to work and felt it was too dangerous for them to live in Bethesda where they were seen as 'traitors'

8

CHAPTER II

WHY BETHESDA REVOLTS

'THE people never rebel from a passion for attack, but from an impatience of suffering.' True of most revolts, these words from the memoirs of Sully (which Mr. John Morley says political students should bind about their necks, and write upon the tables of their hearts) are doubly true of the quarrymen's. As little by little one pieces together the long story of the men's grievances one wonders no longer at their dogged endurance under present sufferings. One marvels instead how the upright, freedom-loving Welshmen ever brought themselves to suffer, even for a day, the sum of indignities and humiliations that marked the late regime. North Wales has been called 'the garden of liberty.' But liberty, happiness, self-respect, all were swallowed up in the 'great hole in the mountain,' whose management offered as great a contrast to ordinary, rational freedom as do the black sides of the quarry to the grandeur of the surrounding mountains. It is not merely that the so-called 'discipline' was degrading to the men; it was, as we shall see, unintelligent – in some cases even childish. To epitomise all the complaints it has produced is impossible. Every quarryman one meets has his individual tale of irritations suffered and endured. These things lie quite outside any formal statement of grievances. But they give a vivid insight into conditions repugnant to Englishmen, and in order that the public may appreciate to the full the species of irritation which the men are combating I proceed to set forth some of these individual complaints. They are representative of many others.

Take first the case of William Evans, the Chairman of the Strike Committee of 1896-1897. Evans applied some time after the strike for an extra day's holiday, not a very immoderate request. It was refused, and Evans appealed, as was his right, from the 'overlooker' to a superior official. The official refused also, and gave as his reason Evans's conduct during the late strike. It is not, perhaps, surprising that Evans

9

characterised this conduct as having 'the appearance of persecution.' Wisdom would have taken no notice of this remark, but Penrhynism and wisdom are not exactly synonymous. In this instance an apology was prepared, which Evans alleges attributed more to him than he actually said. He refused to sign it, and was a little later discharged.

The incident is worthier of the nursery than of a great industry. But it is easy to cap this absurdity with another. A workman at the quarry had a difference as to price with an 'overlooker,' and threatened an appeal to Caesar – his privilege, be it noted, under the settlement of 1897. The overlooker took the bull by the horns, and went straight to a higher official, who sent instantly for the complainant, and met him outside the quarry office. Before the workman had time to speak, however, he was informed that he must consider himself discharged. The man was sent out of the quarry without even being paid the money due to him. He called next day at Port Penrhyn, and was sent with a note back to the quarry. The workman was then paid, and also learnt the nature of his offence. He had appeared, so he was told, 'before his betters with his cap on,' and for that enormity he had been dismissed!

It would be difficult to credit this episode were it not so thoroughly in keeping with a number of other incidents as well substantiated. Take this specimen. Some time after the 1897 strike, an entertainment was given at the market-place, Bethesda, and Lord Penrhyn graciously attended. The officials who acted as stewards did their utmost to make the event a success, and exhausted the resources of Bethesda in decorating the hall. At least two stewards paid in hard cash for their seats, and the seats they selected were, it happened, in front and very near Lord Penrhyn's party. It is really humiliating to have to record the fact that these men, who had a perfect right to sit where they chose, were actually called upon to explain in writing why they had occupied these positions. They returned different answers. One apologised, and was told his letter was 'cringing.' The other, finding the manhood rising in him, answered that he had paid for a seat, and that it was his business which seat he selected. Now, mark the absurdity of what followed. One official was informed that his letter was 'cringing.' The other was rebuked because his letter was 'too independent.'

This is comparatively a trifling incident, but it enables us to form a good idea of the spirit that prevailed at Bethesda. Let me give another complaint of a more serious nature. During the strike of 1897 a deputation of seven men were selected to wait upon Lord Penrhyn. One of these, a certain Robert Thomas, was later interviewing a head official who, he alleges, addressed him thus: "I know you. You mind yourself. You're one of the seven."

It is only fair to Lord Penrhyn to state that this official's services have since been dispensed with (though not in consequence of the men's complaints). But the very fact that it was possible for a responsible official at the quarry to use language like this shows that the men had no security in the individual representation of grievances. It shows that threats and menaces, if not punishment, attended any effort of the men to better their conditions and that, in fact, they were the victims of a petty irritation. Take a further instance. Fourteen men working on a certain spot in the quarry had a grievance and, according to the regulations, appointed a deputation and a spokesman. The spokesman was suspended for a week! His thirteen comrades subscribed among themselves to defray his loss. The reply was a threat to place them under a contractor.

Now these same 'contractors' are a cardinal grievance of the men.

Careful inquiries among all kinds of quarrymen have convinced me that the system of 'contracting,' introduced into the quarry by Lord Penrhyn, affects the question of wages closely. Let me explain first that the system of 'contracts' superseded a system that has obtained in the quarries for decades. The old plan was practically co-operative. Three quarrymen were given a place or 'bargain' in the quarry, and between them hewed down the rock and trimmed it into slates, being paid, of course, by Lord Penrhyn. The new system is to place between men and their employer the middleman, in the shape of a contractor – usually an unskilled labourer in the quarry. The contractor is paid by Lord Penrhyn, who does not – on his own confessing – lose by the innovation. Obviously, therefore, it is from the men that this middleman makes his profit.

It is impossible to conceive of an arrangement more likely to create dissatisfaction. In view of the large output of the quarry, it is impossible to discover any reason for its introduction. The contract system was not the only grievance of the men which touched their earnings. There was an uncertainty about those earnings which must have often galled them almost beyond endurance. The men were paid according to the quality of the piece of rock – the 'bargain,' as it is called – on which they worked. The harder and therefore the more difficult the rock, the more they were paid on every pound of slates made out of it. The quality of the rock – and accordingly the 'poundage' of the men – used to be assessed before work was begun upon it, and the quality of the rock was judged, roughly speaking, by its surface. But the most skilled geologist is sometimes misled by the surface. The rock seems soft, and accordingly the percentage is low; but it turns out after a day or so to be extraordinarily hard. Yet they are still paid a low figure for their pounds of slates. Obviously that is an unsatisfactory and inequitable system. The men paid once a month were never quite sure what they would be able to bring home to their wives at the end of it. The rock might change and their earnings sink to nothing. It was surely not unreasonable, therefore, that they should press for a small minimum wage – a boon already granted in other quarries, and obtaining to-day throughout the quarries of the United States. Lord Penrhyn refused to grant the minimum wage, and gave every evidence that he meant to extend the contract system during the better years between 1897 and 1900.

The men used to return exasperated to their homes. Nearly every day they were working under unskilled men, who bullied them and paid them unfairly, and they were working with no reasonable certainty as to their earnings. They were free to complain individually, but to do so was to court dismissal. It is this kind of treatment which has made the quarrymen passionately wedded to the idea of combination, or at least to the idea of a committee who could represent to the management the grievances which so exasperated them during the years I have mentioned – grievances which they still speak of with a bitterness that time cannot efface.

These grievances, the men allege, cannot be properly represented under the present quarry regulations. Hence their request for a reinstatement of the old Quarry Committee which Lord Penrhyn abolished in 1884. True, Clause I of the 1897 agreement – signed by Lord Penrhyn after the last strike – does provide for the representation of grievances – after a fashion. But it insists that before a general deputation representing all the men wait upon the management there shall be a sectional deputation from the grade affected. This seems far more innocuous than it really is. To the outsider it may appear to leave the men free to urge redress of grievances. But, in actual fact, it makes it virtually impossible for them to do so. And for two simple reasons. The average monoglot quarryman is quite capable, in his simple, unsophisticated manner, of stating his own grievance, and of making it understood. But he is no more capable of debating it point by point with Mr. Young, than he would be of arguing with the law Lords on an appeal case. It is not his business to fence with words, but to hew wealth out of rock hard as the management heart, and it has frequently happened that in various sections there are not the requisite six men who feel disposed to 'stand up' to Lord Penrhyn or Mr. Young for an hour and a half. Those who have endured the ordeal will appreciate their hesitancy. What match is the average quarryman, slow of thought and of speech, for Mr. Young who has a plausible, but not convincing reason, ready for every defect that can be urged against his management? In a bout of words it takes the men's leaders all their time to make their points clear without being overborne. The rank and file of the quarrymen would stand no chance whatever.

Moreover, the rank and file do not feel that confidence in the management which permits of the individual or sectional representation of grievances. Over and over again, men who thus presented complaints have found themselves discharged without hope of re-engagement or work, for, by a solemn covenant, quarry proprietors in North Wales are bound not to engage discharged employees. The men, in short, have no confidence in any method that does not present the cause of one quarryman as the cause of all – the principle which lies at the very root of combination.

How vitally important that principle is to the men, the following incident shows: – In 1884 a deputation from them waited on the present Lord Penrhyn, then the Hon. George Sholto Douglas Pennant. That high-minded and chivalrous aristocrat heard their leaders' statements, and then, calling the three Unionist members of the deputation before him, he read out to them a peremptory notice of dismissal. These men had worked in the quarry all their lives, and not a single complaint had ever been made against their work or their character. Two of them had worked in the quarry for over thirty years. So great was the indignation roused among the men by this savage act that they threatened to strike if their leaders were not reinstated. Nominally this was done, but the Unionists were marked men. They were told that the managers would be specially desired to report on their future conduct.

True, this took place so far back as 1884, but that Penrhynism has not changed its spots since then, the cases quoted above conclusively show. Lord Penrhyn is still adamant as regards combination. He does not explicitly 'deny' it to his workmen. He merely refuses to recognise the only practical embodiment that combination can take. Let there be no doubt upon this point. It is one of cardinal importance, and I propose to call Lord Penrhyn himself as a witness. Speaking to the deputation of March 27th, 1897, he said:

'With regard to what you say about the Union making the cause of one man the cause of all, that is the trades union principle, I believe, and I have nothing to do, and do not wish to have anything to do, with attempting to interfere with your right in that matter: all that I do object to is a committee which attempts to interfere between master and man.

'Mr. W. H. Williams: We do not get a reply from your lordship in your saying that you do not interfere. When your lordship says you are not going to interfere, there is no answer to the question. What we ask is whether, when the grievance of one is taken up by the others, will the representatives of the men be accepted to deal with that matter before the management?

'Lord Penrhyn: Any man who has a complaint can bring it forward by deputation.

'Mr. W. H. Williams: But a deputation could not take up the grievance of a man unless there was a committee in existence, which would be in a position to consider whether his grievance was such as to be taken up by all the men.

'Lord Penrhyn: There is nothing to prevent a man consulting his fellow-workmen in the quarry as to whether his case ought to be heard or not.

'Mr. W. H. Williams: But we cannot do that without a committee.

'Lord Penrhyn: There may be, as you know, any number of committees in the quarry, so long as they do not interfere with the management.

'Mr. W. H. Williams: We do not ask that they should be permitted to manage the quarry. All we ask is that the Committee should be permitted to consider whether a single workman receives injustice, and if the Committee arrive at the decision that such workman is receiving injustice, that the Committee, as such, should have a right to send a deputation to the manager with reference to that man's case, so that the deputation will emanate from the Committee.

'Lord Penrhyn: So that the complaint shall come from the Committee?

'Mr. W. H. Williams: Yes.

'Lord Penrhyn: And not in consequence of an individual complaint?

'Mr. W. H. Williams: As the result, my lord, of a complaint by a single individual, which the Committee, after taking up, has made a subject concerning all; so that the deputation would approach the manager with a grievance, which by this time had become the property of the Committee, and not the grievance of a single individual, although he might have been the cause or origin of it?

'Lord Penrhyn: Then you wish me to acknowledge a sort of Standing Committee in the quarry? Is that what I understand?

'Mr. W. H. Williams: Exactly so, my lord, but not to manage the work.

'Lord Penrhyn: Then for what purpose?

'Mr. W. H. Williams: To discuss grievances with the management.

'Mr. E. A. Young: To stand between the men and the management.

'Mr. W. H. Williams: It is not between the men and the management. The Committee are the men pressed into a small compass – in the form of a Committee.'

Can anything be plainer or more explicit than the men's modest and reasonable demands? Could anything be more disingenuous than the position Lord Penrhyn chose to take up, the position he takes up now? Is it not fatuous to formally admit the 'right' of the men to combine, and then refuse to allow the simplest application of that right? Is there anyone who is deceived by so transparent a device?

The fact is that Lord Penrhyn presents grossly and palpably the old feudal view – the Divine right of the landlord to do what he likes with his own. The men who are suffering to-day urge that it is their skill and toil which give value to the quarry, and surely they have some claim to control the conditions of their own labour. It is, in fact, a natural fight between the old idea and the new – a perfectly typical phrase of the great world conflict of our time, but for sheer picturesqueness and tragic intensity of interest, the conditions of the fight have never been approached.

A busy scene near the Waterloo Hotel on Bethesda High Street

A few soldiers standing idly on Bethesda High Street during the Strike

16

CHAPTER III

'POLICE!'

BETHESDA'S ordeal does not end with starvation. As I have said the quarrymen have suffered ceaseless persecution at the hands of the police. The quarrymen, I need hardly say, are ordinarily law-abiding and peaceable to a degree. Before the strike commenced one sergeant and two constables were more than sufficient to control this crimeless community, and it was rare indeed for any serious charge to be preferred against the men or their families. Obviously these are not the kind of men to harbour any wild anarchic objections to law and order, and it has been impossible, therefore, for me to dismiss as so much mere idle talk their frequently reiterated complaints against the constabulary. I have made careful inquiries into these complaints, and I regret to say that they disclose a highly unsatisfactory state of things. What are the facts in question? I shall state, first, those which have been sworn to in open court, and decided upon by the magistrates. I have said that the Bangor Bench have, upon occasions, in effect condemned the police. Let me give an instance:

On September 3rd one William Hughes, a striker, was charged with resisting the police in the execution of their duty, and also with assaulting a constable. The case was a remarkable one. Hughes swore that some constables first followed and then pushed him down and struck him; that, further, they placed a handcuff on his wrist and twisted his arm as they marched him off to the station. His statement was supported by witnesses, and despite the evidence of five constables who had arrested him, the Bench elected to believe the prisoner, who was discharged. Now, according to the very testimony that secured his dismissal, Hughes had been the victim of a gratuitous arrest and gross cruelty. Yet, strange to state, no steps were taken by the authorities, and the policemen whose testimony had been disregarded by the magistrates were not even censured. They are still members of the force, and their evidence is still being taken. I need hardly say that if ever a case called for inquiry, it was this one. It does not stand alone. A woman named Ellen Hughes was some time back charged with rioting. The police evidence was very definite, and she was committed to the Assizes at Carnarvon. A constable swore most positively that not merely had he seen her behaving in a disorderly manner, but that he had followed her into a shop and cautioned her, before taking her into custody. What are we to think of the value of police evidence in this district when I say that the defence produced the actual alleged rioter, the very woman who had been cautioned by the constable, and who bore not the slightest resemblance to the prisoner? That the constable committed perjury I do not for a moment suggest, but I imagine that if such a breakdown occurred in a case promoted by the London police an official inquiry would inevitably take place forthwith.

It has been frequently stated in open court that many of the 'bradyrs' brandish loaded revolvers of an evening – for which, by the way, they have no licence whatever. Attention has been frequently directed to this disgraceful state of things, which might easily lead to loss of life. Incredible as it may seem, no action has been taken, although the danger to the community is further increased by the fact that many of the 'bradyrs' are, as I can testify, frequently drunk. As the police themselves have shown no disposition to remove this public danger, the attention of the Home Secretary is, I understand, to be directed to it. But it illustrates an attitude which is one of the factors in the situation.

When Messrs. Carter, Vincent, and Co., solicitors to Lord Penrhyn, prosecuted some strikers at Carnarvon, it was the same firm who, as Acting Under-Sheriff for the county, empanelled the jury! The Judge promptly quashed the panel; but, unfortunately, a bench of magistrates is not made of the same stuff as a Judge of the High Court.

Let me give a further illustration of the police attitude. I was present in court the other day when a 'bradyr' was fined and bound over for an absolutely unprovoked assault on a man who was not even a striker. The prosecution was very ably and quite fairly conducted by a superintendent who, however, forgot to tell the Bench what most of those in court knew, that the prisoner had been twice brought before them on similar charges. Had he done so, the young man must have been sent to prison.

I have before me the letter of a Free Church minister, in which he repeats a grave statement which he had thought fit to make concerning a police-constable. He alleges that he found the constable beating a child, that he first remonstrated with him, and then reported him to his sergeant. The sergeant pleaded for mercy for the man, and promised the minister to rebuke the errant constable and to change his beat. This was done, but the constable was again found by one of the best-known tradesmen in Bethesda beating another child. The facts were made known to the Chief Constable who, let it be said to his credit, himself inquired into them. But if anything was done to caution the constable it had singularly little effect, for I have evidence of a recent instance of exactly similar conduct on the part of the same officer.

Let me explain in connection with these beatings that policemen in Bethesda are armed usually with stout walking-sticks. Occasionally when the outcry against the use which they make of these has been particularly strong, they have been deprived of the weapons. But the relief is a short one for Bethesda. Some of the constables are, of course, civil and reliable fellows; some, I regret to say, however, are gratuitously uncivil. They parade the High Street with a swagger, and are as complete a contrast to the Metropolitan Police as I can imagine. There is no charge too petty to prefer against a striker, and a considerable aggregate sum has been expended by the men in defending these persecuting prosecutions. I need hardly say how it exasperates the patient, law-abiding quarrymen to be continually harassed, and to have this unfair annoyance added to their many trials. That the police have difficulties to face no one can deny, but with tact and freedom from prejudice these should be honourably surmounted. The worst result is that, as I have had occasion to remark, the strikers prefer to suffer assault rather than run the risk of an abortive prosecution. The slowness of the Bangor Bench to convict in the case of a 'bradyr' is only equalled by their rapidity of decision when a striker is in the dock. An instance of this rises to my mind. Last Christmas a striker returning home late at night was, he alleges, struck by a constable and severely injured. He knocked up a doctor, who found him bleeding profusely. Afterwards the man saw a minister who, with the doctor, gave evidence against the constable. There does not seem much doubt, therefore, as to the reality of the assault. Yet the Bench, on such overwhelming evidence as this, could not agree!

The Committee of Inquiry, appointed by the Carnarvonshire County Council to inquire into the above and other charges against the constabulary, have found, by a majority of five to two, that the police acted without due regard to the feelings or the 'liberties' of the strikers. They also condemn the force on other grounds, and recommend the removal to other districts of two important officers. This is a complete vindication of *The Daily News'* criticism of the constabulary and will, we may take it, effectually protect the strikers from similar gross abuses. News comes to me as I pass the proof of these words that the report has been adopted by the Police Committee of the Council, after a protracted and heated debate, by a majority of two to one! On which *The Daily News* observes – and I can make no better comment – 'We may hope that the police tyranny at Bethesda is at an end.' It is well, however, that the facts should be recorded.

CHAPTER IV

SIXTY YEARS OF PENRHYNISM

HISTORY repeats itself. I am turning aside for the moment from the task of chronicling the daily waste and wear of this terrible industrial tragedy, with its thousand and one concomitant evils, to give, if only in outline, the past history of Penrhynism. That insight is absolutely necessary if one is to read the present situation aright. It cannot be too clearly understood that Bethesda's revolt is not a thing of yesterday. For the last century this patient effort of a fine race to achieve emancipation from intolerable conditions has been going on, and at least four generations of quarrymen have fought against the regime Lord Penrhyn still supports. The story of this struggle for freedom has rarely been equalled for pathos and interest. To tell it in detail would be impossible, but I set out below, some of the more typical incidents. Those show convincingly what it is of supreme importance for the public to grasp – that, so far from the men being fractious and undisciplined, a prey to agitators, and prone to rebellion, they are in reality patient to a fault, suffering with too much forbearance indignities and humiliations such as no other body of workers have in our time endured.

Let me quote first from a remonstrance addressed by the men to Lord Penrhyn's predecessor, so far back as 1825. It commences, 'Honoured Sir,' and it goes on in simple, unaffected language (of which I give an almost literal translation), 'to beg in the most humble manner for your permission to inform you that we are not able to work for the wages paid to us hitherto, because it is impossible for us to live upon them.'

'We, the quarrymen and labourers in your employ' (the remonstrance continues), 'beg to inform you that we do not get fair play. Our only reason for being on strike is that you should know we experience a deal of tyranny. Many men, considered to be the best

21

quarrymen in the quarry, have not earned more lately than 17s per month. Others have earnt from £5 to £6 per month. When fellow-workers are in partnership, and take a bargain, and commence operations within a few yards of each other, and earn not more than 17s; whilst others, working on the same rock, earn five times as much, then it cannot be that justice is being done. We only want to be dealt with fairly and impartially, and not to work for less than 3/9 a day, we to supply our own tools and powder. Further, we do not wish to work under some of the officials now engaged, and we hope that your honour will pardon us for addressing you thus, and that you will inquire into the cause of our grievances.'

It is difficult to translate into smooth English this rough, but earnest, plea for justice. My translation shows however that then, as now, the men were only too willing to accept any small instalment of equity. Then, as now, so far from being truculent and aggressive, they were humble and conciliatory. Then, as now, they complained of the bullying and nepotism of officials, and of an utterly unfair, indeed, a capricious, system of remuneration; and then, as now, their reasonable remonstrance was met by an exactly opposite spirit.

Twenty years later we find the men again in revolt. The effort was only spasmodic, but it served to bring out some of the worst features of Penrhynism. Its story has been powerfully told in a letter written many years later by a victimised leader of the men, an exile that the regime of the quarry drove from home. His narrative throbs with human interest, and I need make no apology for quoting from it:

'It was in August, 1845,' he writes, 'that, whilst I was working in the double gallery, a young man of the name of Harry Ishmael came to me, with a slate on which was written a notice inviting the quarrymen to come out on strike on a certain day at 12 o'clock. I read the notice, and the news spread like wildfire through all the sheds. The men thronged to where I stood. The question now was to get someone to take the slate bearing the message to the gallery above. I volunteered, though some tried to dissuade me. I said, "My friends, don't stand in the way of the gospel" (*Efengyl*, literally 'good news'). I carried the slate to the gallery above ... The day of the strike came, and the scene was terrible. A thousand men stood waiting on the edge of the galleries, looking down into the bottom of the quarry where they had been summoned. For a moment all hesitated; the silence got fearful.

Suddenly a start was made. The men commenced coming down, and their numbers swelled instantly. From gallery to gallery they came down, shouting and rejoicing.'

The strike had begun! But this picture of revolt was soon blotted out. The men gave way 'on terms' next day.

'Peace followed' (the exile's letter continues), 'and no one thought any further notice would be taken. But on the morning of the second day I was told that some Judas had put Thomas Hughes on the scent regarding the carrying of the message, and that the scent was being followed from gallery to gallery. Before midday Hughes came to me with a man and asked if it was true that I had given him the slate. I answered "Yes." The next thing to know was who had given the slate to me. I replied I did not know. He tried in vain to get the name from me, but I refused.'

As a result the man's lot became unbearable. He was put on starvation wages, and at last he resolved to quit the quarry. Thus he tells the story:

'I put my case before my best friends, and we concluded that my days at the Quarry were numbered, and advised me to go thence. I resolved to go to America, and my friends collected £8 for me. Three pounds I paid as my fare in a slate vessel from Bangor to Boston, kept one pound in my pocket, and gave the rest to my mother, when I kissed her for the last time. I shall never forget her last words to me. Through her tears she said, "My boy, I shall never see you again".'

The writer of this letter is still alive. He has flourished exceedingly since Penrhynism made him an exile. But can any prosperity compensate him for that last view of his mother, whom he was to see during all the years that followed broken and in misery at the loss of her son?

The case of this exile does not stand alone. All these revolts had their victims, and all left their marks on the men. Well might the writer of this letter add, 'There is fire in every tear begotten by tyranny.' The men were beaten, but not broken. They rebelled again and again.

I pass over many of these revolts covering a period of thirty years. During this time the owner of the quarries threatened eviction of the men 'if they had anything to do with such a movement as a trade union.' In 1875 the quarrymen braved that threat, and, thanks largely to the untiring energy and courage of Mr. W. J. Parry, the Quarrymen's

Union was floated. At Dinorwic quarries two thousand men were asked, 'What is your choice? You must give up your union or your job.' They answered boldly, 'We will stick to the union.' The Penrhyn helots caught the infection of freedom, and subscribed £250 for their comrades. They did more. They rallied as one man to the union, and won their first great signal victory. They forced a recognition of the Quarry Committee from the late Lord Penrhyn, and they got control of their own Sick and Benefit Club.

So far, so good. But mark well what immediately followed in this latter connection. The victory of the men included an investigation into the Benefit Club's accounts, and the discovery was actually made, and is now on record, that there was a shortage of over two thousand pounds in the club's accounts, a shortage the late Lord Penrhyn was compelled to make up! What can be said for a system that compels men to subscribe to a fund that denies them the right of controlling its finances, and then does not even see that the books are properly kept? A more striking example of the inefficiency resultant on treating men as machines could not be forthcoming.

But for some that method still has, it seems, its attractions. Ten years after this discovery the present lord assumed control of the quarry. The men's victory was undone. Their charter of privileges was taken from them, the old bad system was re-established. An incident occurred which, though I have narrated it before, so vividly illustrates that system, that I state it again. A deputation waited on Lord Penrhyn to urge redress of alleged grievances. Lord Penrhyn encouraged his men to present these by dismissing three members of the deputation on the spot! True the men were afterwards re-engaged, but only on terms invidious to themselves.

Of such is the character of Penrhynism. The four examples I have selected show clearly the character of the long struggle of which the present dispute is only the latest phase. On the one side, as we may see, there is a tradition of persecution, of arbitrary dismissals, of coercion, threats, and penalties. On the other side, we have the patient diffidence of the men, reluctant to offend, but borne up by a religious hatred of the regime they have resisted for over a century, the regime they are at last fully resolved to end.

As I have said, history repeats itself – but always with a difference. This time there will be no half measures. It is a fight to a finish. If the men surrender they will go in utterly beaten and crushed. Lord Penrhyn's victory will be decisive. It will need another generation of quarrymen to arise before the fight is renewed. But, if the men conquer this time, then we may take it that the reign of Penrhynism will be over. The last survival of the feudal system will have been carried, and a fine race will have achieved its liberation.

Penrhyn v. Parry. September 8, 1903. W. J. Parry and the Defence Fund Committee
Back row (from left): R. W. Roberts, H. M. Roberts, D. H. Jones, R. Edwards, Isaac Davies
Middle row: H. Hughes, John Jones, W. George, W. J. Parry, Charles Sheridan Jones, W. W. Lloyd, E. R. Jones
Seated, front: R. D. Griffith, R. D. Williams, Lewis Jones

CHAPTER V

THE PENRHYN LAND SYSTEM

FREQUENTLY the question is asked, Why do not the men seek other masters? The answer is easily stated. For decades past the aim of the Penrhyn policy has been to tie the people to the place.

For some days past I have been investigating at first hand some of the results of the Penrhyn policy regarding land. The experience has been a curious one. Study the Penrhyn system of land tenure, and you will be tempted to despair of reason and justice. Under it, the most striking qualities of the quarrymen are perverted. The love of home, of peace and quietude, which marks this fine race in a generation of sensation-mongers, their deep religious sentiment, the very labour and skill of their own hands, all these things enslave them.

The land system, in fact, is the corner-stone of Penrhynism, and without it the present lord could never have withstood the men's demand for justice. But for its provisions, the quarries would have been idle years ago, or would have been worked only under equitable conditions. The system deprives the men of labour's chief protection – mobility. Denied fair play in one district, the average artisan can get it in another. Not so the Penrhyn quarrymen. They are bound hand and foot to Bethesda, and are thus absolutely dependent on Lord Penrhyn!

So much for its general effect. Let us now consider this pernicious system in detail.

Right at the top of Llandegai Mountain, towering over the south side of Bethesda, is a miniature estate of quarrymen's cottages, exquisite with a certain trim simplicity that I find it impossible to describe, and commanding a magnificent view of the surrounding country. The story of these cottages, and how they came to be erected, illustrates vividly the leading features of the Penrhyn land system, and is besides full of interest. I propose, therefore, to briefly set it forth.

Sixty years ago Llandegai Mountain was rough, hard rocky land, without roads or fertilization, and with only a handful of scattered houses.

The land, when used at all, was used only for sheep and cattle, and it was universally regarded, and, I have no doubt whatever, rightly regarded, as common land. Let that point pass for the moment, however, and let us consider the transformation that took place in the next few years. Men were needed to develop the quarries, and those men had to be provided with additional houses. Lord Penrhyn's predecessor took the opportunity to inaugurate a system of masterly ingenuity. He seized Llandegai Mountain, laid it out in roads, and graciously gave permission to the men to build themselves cottages upon it; that is to say, upon the land which was as much theirs as his own. He did more. He granted the men leases, upon terms I shall presently explain, and he appointed Mr. Francis, the manager of the quarry, to look after the estate also.

It is not difficult to catch the significance of this appointment. To differ from Mr. Francis in his capacity as estate agent meant dismissal from the quarry. The only way, in fact, in which a quarryman could get taken on 'at the great hole in the mountain' was by submitting absolutely to his master's will and pleasure as regards the tenure of his house. The men were caught in a double trap. If they rebelled as quarrymen, they were soon made to suffer as tenants. If they objected as tenants to the terms of their leases, they were dismissed from the quarry. As matters stood, they were in need of two things – first, they needed work whereby they could live, and secondly they required house room. Lord Penrhyn's predecessor enjoyed a virtual monopoly of both, and, having these, he held the men in the hollow of his hand. Many quarrymen had come to Bethesda from far-off parts of the country. They had either to leave their families from week-end to week-end, and put up with poor lodgings in Bethesda, or to close on such terms for new accommodation as the quarry manager chose to offer. They took the latter course.

They worked literally day and night to get the cottages erected. Long after their day's work at the quarry was ended, right on till ten and twelve o'clock at night, they continued doggedly building their future homes out of rough slate slabs and rock. The only part of these cottages, as far as I have been able to ascertain, not wholly the result of their own labour are the roofs, which in some cases the management supplied, and it says much for the skill and ingenuity of these men that these houses, after sixty years of wear and tear, still stand solid and flawless, infinitely superior to the jerry-built hovels the town-worker knows too well. That these cottages have endured is not, however, surprising. They were cemented literally by the very life-blood of the strong men who built them. The strain of working all day in the quarry, and then for hours on hours building with rough and insufficient tools, proved too much for most of them. The majority died off while still in the prime of life. Few survived to old age. They left little behind them but a shelter for their wives and children – and that shelter, be it noted, the shelter that they built, Lord Penrhyn owns to-day.

The terms on which the men were granted leases for the homes they themselves put up upon land that, as I have said, Lord Penrhyn did not own, were instructive and peculiar. The leases were granted only for thirty years. But in many cases the actual lease was not delivered until years after the tenant took possession. All that was given was a permission to build, and thus the quarrymen were made to feel more than ever dependent on Lord Penrhyn. And the position to-day of the present tenants is no better.

It is not merely that they pay increasingly large rents for the cottages their fathers and grandfathers built, but they are denied rights enjoyed in every part of the kingdom. Let me give an instance. Some time ago Mr. William Jones, M.P., desired to address his constituents of Llandegai Mountain. He found he could not do so. There were chapels, there were farm buildings, in which a meeting could have been suitably held, but the Penrhyn leases forbade. And, finally, this distinguished man, who is heard with delight every time he rises in the House of Commons, had to speak to a handful of his constituents from the roadside. If any of the residents of Llandegai Mountain desire to discuss parochial matters, it is to the roadside that they must repair. The Penrhyn leases, in fact, make discussion of political questions, or of grievances, or of the strike, virtually impossible. Hanging over the head of every tenant is the possibility of eviction from the house his father built.

So far as Llandegai is concerned, in view of the special circumstances of the case, that possibility may appear a little remote. But Llandegai only differs from the rest of the Penrhyn estate as regards the alienation of common land. Everywhere the broad facts are the same.

The men have built upon leases. They are tied down to the place for years. Then, if their lease is not renewed, they have the possibility of eviction staring them in the face. Some, it is true, are freeholders, and their position in the present dispute is ironical indeed. They own a house – and it is valueless. As one of them crudely but forcibly put it to me, "It is food I want, not a house. I cannot let or sell my house any more than I can eat it."

Let us consider some of the figures of the Penrhyn leasehold system. As I have said, the land on which many of the cottages stand was swampy and rocky ground, not worth sixpence an acre. The ground rent charged for this was ten shillings a plot. When the leases fell in, the rents were increased to three or four pounds. The more the tenant had expended in keeping his cottage in good repair the more he is charged when the lease ends!

As with the quarrymen's houses, so with larger buildings. One house near Bethesda, standing on three and a half acres of ground, cost £3000 to erect. The land was rough and rocky, and was let for about two pounds an acre. The ground rent of £12 per annum will amount during the eighty years of the lease to £960, for land that sold in the open market would probably not have fetched more than £150; while the £3000 the lessee expended will, at the expiration of the lease, pass out of the control of his successors. If ever there was a place which showed the evils of the present leasehold system, it is Bethesda.

To-day, if the men leave their cottages, they must surrender the savings of years, they must turn their back on the little cottage which they have felt throughout their lives was their own, and which their fathers built at so dreadful an expense. Some have made the wrench. In unspeakable bitterness of spirit they have gone from Bethesda, never to return. But the great bulk remains, and looks with confidence to the most generous and determined nation in the world, the nation that never failed to appreciate a good fight, to "see them through."

CHAPTER VI

WHERE IS THE BOARD OF TRADE?

ON the 6th of December last the sorely-tried quarrymen made their last effort to bring their long struggle to a close. Lord Penrhyn had left their letter unanswered. He was clearly implacable. The whole district was threatened, nay faced, with ruin, and the men's leaders felt that on them rested the obligation of exhausting all other possibilities of settlement, and accordingly they applied to the Board of Trade to put in force its powers under the Conciliation Act, 1896, powers which are defined in the following terms:

Under the significant heading of 'Powers of Board of Trade as to trade disputes,' Sec. 2, Sub-sec, I, declares that:

'1. Where a difference exists or is apprehended between an employer, or any class of employers, and workmen, or between different classes of workmen, the Board of Trade may, if they think fit, exercise all or any of the following powers, namely, –

(a) inquire into the causes and circumstances of the difference;

(b) take such steps as to the Board may seem expedient for the purpose of enabling the parties to the difference to meet together, by themselves or their representatives, under the presidency of a chairman mutually agreed upon, or nominated by the Board of Trade or by some other person or body, with a view to the amicable settlement of the difference;

(c) on the application of employers or workmen interested, and after taking into consideration the existence and adequacy of means available for conciliation in the district or trade and the circumstances of the case, appoint a person or persons to act as conciliator or as a board of conciliation.

2. If any person is so appointed to act as conciliator, he shall inquire into the causes and circumstances of the difference by communication with the parties, and otherwise shall endeavour to bring about a

settlement of the difference, and shall report his proceedings to the Board of Trade.'

The men had an easy task in showing that their quarrel lay well within the scope the legislature had intended this clause should have. They pointed to the widespread misery caused by the dispute, and to the fact that, to the appeals of the Carnarvonshire County Council, as to their own, Lord Penrhyn had turned a deaf ear. Their request was in every respect reasonable. Since the Conciliation Act was passed there have been no less than 130 applications under it. Seventy of these disputes the Board has settled. In thirty-three instances only has failure attended its efforts. But, in almost every case except the quarrymen's, the Board has at least tried to effect a settlement. It is difficult to discover any creditable reason why the quarrymen should have been an exception to this excellent rule. None the less that exception was made, and on December the 19th, *two days before the rising of Parliament*, Mr. Gerald Balfour refused to lift a finger to do what it was clearly well within the functions of his office to effect. Comparisons are odious, but I cannot offer any better comment on this flagrant failure of a Minister to do his plain duty than the following leader from *The Daily News*, contrasting the inertia of a *doctrinaire*, with the vigour of a robust statesman: –

'It is a pity that we cannot have something of Mr. Roosevelt's spirit at the English Board of Trade. The President of the United States has called down upon himself the fury of the coal-owners by daring to interfere in a dispute which these gentlemen consider as a matter between themselves and their workpeople alone. In this country a struggle of much the same sort, though, happily, of less serious moment to the nation as a whole, has been dragging on for nearly two years and what has the Board of Trade done, or attempted to do? The answer is that it has done nothing whatever. For all that the public know of the matter, Mr. Gerald Balfour has never heard of the war at Bethesda, and if this terrible and tragic chapter in our industrial history is considered beneath the notice of the Department immediately concerned with industrial disputes, it goes without saying that the Government have never given it a moment's consideration. Mr. Ritchie, indeed, has sent troops to overawe the wives and children of the quarrymen, but that is the measure of the Government's solicitude. And Mr. Gerald Balfour cannot plead that he has no means of intervention at his disposal. The Conciliation Act of 1896 was passed by a Ministry in which he held office, and it is frequently brought into use for the adjustment of strikes up and down the country. That Act, as our Special Commissioner shows to-day, is something more than an instrument for bringing together the parties to a dispute who are already in a mood for conciliation. It enables the Board of Trade to appoint a conciliator, who shall inquire into the causes and circumstances of the difference, and endeavour to bring about a settlement of the dispute, and this official is charged to report his proceedings to the Board of Trade. Why is it that Mr. Balfour has taken no steps to put this part of the Act into operation? Is he afraid of encountering a rebuff from a single Peer, whilst Mr. Roosevelt is willing to face the wrath of one of the most powerful of American monopolies, and to estrange at the same time the whole body of organised financiers, railway companies, and manufacturers, who see in the intervention of the head of the State a menace to their claim to do what they will with their own? Mr. Balfour may possibly plead that the results of the late Sir Courtenay Boyle's attempts to bring Lord Penrhyn to reason during the strike in the 'nineties were of no avail. But the failure of the Board of Trade in the past is no reason why the State should lie down to be trampled on by Lord Penrhyn to-day, and if Mr. Balfour has no better reason to offer for his policy of *laissez faire* his case is not a strong one. His business, we may remind him, is to put the law in motion; it is for the country to judge what further steps should be taken if it turns out that the law is insufficient to meet the requirements of the hour. A Minister who refuses to exercise the powers which he possesses is, it seems to us, a less creditable figure than the policeman who skulks in a side street when there is rioting on his beat. That is not Mr. Roosevelt's way. The President goes straight to the centre of the disturbance without stopping to consider questions of dignity and the like. But, then, Mr. Roosevelt conceives himself to be the servant of the State, and not of the interests.

'Now, the Penrhyn struggle happens to raise issues which are just as momentous to the State as the claim of the Pennsylvania masters to exercise their stewardship without regard to the public convenience or the rights of labour. Indeed, neither the anthracite kings nor the owner of the slate quarries recognise any such stewardship, and it is precisely in their incapacity to gauge the conditions of tenure which modern civilization imposes upon them that the danger to society lies. Neither

Lord Penrhyn nor the American magnates who are fighting so fiercely for the destruction of the miners' unions understand that the State which guarantees them in the enjoyment of their property is bound to safeguard its own interests and to find means for keeping the Commonwealth factor paramount. This lesson Mr. Roosevelt is endeavouring, though without immediate success, to impress upon the American mine owners and workmen, and we imagine that so soon as Mr. Mitchell and the miners are satisfied that they will be secured in the rights of combination, the end of the crisis will be in sight. The danger here is that a similar assertion of the rights of the State as against the claims to personal despotism will not be made, or even attempted. The first thing, it seems to us, is to bring home to the Government their responsibility under the Conciliation Act, and an opportunity will no doubt be found soon after the House of Commons assembles for the Session. In the meantime, the Bethesda quarrymen will not be deserted by those who believe in the justice of their claims.'

CHAPTER VII

A ROCK OF DELIVERANCE

'WOULD not this seem a very good opportunity to acquire and start a Co-operative Quarry? It seems to me that this is just what might be made into a most successful object-lesson as to what co-operation among the workers would effect.' Thus said Lady Warwick; and in view of the facts I set forth below these words have especial interest for all friends of the quarrymen. There are quite close to Bethesda three quarries – the Tanybolch, Pantreiniog, and Moel Faban. Tanybolch, I am assured by those who speak with authority, it would be profitless to develop, and it is now disused. But Moel Faban and Pantreiniog are both being worked, and are both yielding a profit, though in both cases operations are hampered by lack of capital. It is claimed, and the belief is strongly held in the district, that, with adequate capital, work could be found at the former quarry for several hundred men, and handsome profits at the same time could be secured. Without committing myself to any conclusion on the matter, I propose to state the grounds of this belief.

First, let me point out that so far as Moel Faban is concerned, it is not merely Bethesda which should have an interest in its development. The mountain, in which the quarry has been cut, is Crown land, and is virtually the property of the nation, to whose exchequer any income derived from it is paid. Surely it is profoundly unsatisfactory, therefore, that the nation should be left in complete ignorance as to the value of its property. Here is a mountain which, according to common report in the district, a district where geologists are plentiful, is 'full of slate,' and on which thousands of pounds, it is said, could be profitably expended.

For some years Moel Faban has been practically under the control of an enterprising Bethesda tradesman, who secured a 'take-note' from the Crown agent nearly two decades ago. Hampered by lack of capital,

35

he has been content to keep two or three men in constant employment at the quarry. Here I found them the other day, cross-cutting the slates that they had hewn down from the sides. According to the figures supplied me, the yearly yield averages 23,325 'best' slates, 20,700 'seconds,' 4300 'thirds,' and 2960 'green' slates. On these there is a profit of fifty per cent. on the small working expenses. I examined some of the slates resting in upright rows on the mountain top. They are, to all appearance, of identically the same quality as the famous Penrhyn blue slates, and the geological theory is that the Penrhyn vein runs through the mountain, which stands exactly opposite the great quarry.

This, of itself, is slight foundation for the liberal expectations that have been formed in the neighbourhood. But there are other facts. That there is slate of marketable quality in the mountain the quarry itself shows. This slate is close to the surface, and crops up everywhere on the two hundred and sixty-five acres comprising the Crown land. But, what is more important, a tunnel was some years ago driven into the side of the mountain for a distance of about one hundred and twenty yards. This tunnel I have explored. As on the surface, so here, thirty and forty yards down, I found slate, which my companions, who could fairly claim to be practical geologists, alleged was marketable, and with plenty of those natural joints that make it easy to cut down.

The ideal method, of course, of developing the Crown lands would be for the Carnarvonshire County Council to promote a Bill in Parliament for powers to work them. The matter has been seriously discussed in the district, but the prospect of converting the Welsh farmer, conservative and unenterprising to a degree, to this form of municipal Socialism has daunted the boldest spirits there. It would be very interesting if the Cooperative Societies, who with their enormous resources have made even larger experiments, were to take the question of these quarries into consideration. But, in any case, whatever be the outcome, it is important that the facts should no longer remain unknown outside the district.

Feeling locally runs strongly in favour of a Cooperative effort. It is felt that the men who are going to work the quarry should have some interest in the profits. No doubt it would be simpler were some millionaire to drop from the clouds, to persuade him to write a cheque, and open the quarry forthwith. But millionaires are scarce in Wales, and the simple, freedom-loving quarryman does not take kindly to their pursuit. Instead he has, greatly daring, resolved to see if it is possible to open the quarry on the lines of labour co-partnership.

There is no doubt that this is a bold aim, but much can be said in its favour. To begin with, the individual capitalist, the only practical alternative, may get drawn into the vicious whirlpool, of which Penrhynism is the vortex. Already nine out of ten quarry proprietors in North Wales are united against labour. It would be worse than useless to open up another quarry if it is to become merely another entrenchment for the enemy. On the other hand, the application of the co-partnership system would not merely give the individual quarryman an exceptional interest in his work, but it would permit of his having some control over the conditions of his own labour, and would be a strong guarantee against the recurrence of these chronic conflicts between quarry proprietors and their employees. The co-partnership principle, in fact, has exactly those qualities which are fitted to meet the difficulties of the case. It would give permanence and strength to the venture, and would reconcile those antagonisms which have cost the quarry industry so dear.

And, on a small scale, the co-partnership principle could be applied immediately. There are still some of the old guards at Bethesda, who have a portion of their savings intact. These they would cheerfully sink in the certainty of regular employment. The aggregate sum that these veterans could plank down would be but a mere bagatelle, of course, compared to what is required. Not less than thirty thousand pounds will suffice to open up Moel Faban on an extensive scale, but of this money only one-third would be wanted forthwith. The balance will not be required until the galleries are opened out and the number of men at work increased considerably. Ten thousand pounds, then, is wanted for immediate purposes, and those who are chiefly interested in the matter at Bethesda are setting themselves to the task of raising the money. It should by no means be beyond their power. The quarrymen have many and powerful friends. Nearly every town has its knot of sympathisers, as the receipts of the choirs and the subscription lists attest. And apart from the well-to-do sympathisers, it is felt that the required capital is only a flea-bite to the great co-operative societies, many of whom have hundreds of thousands of pounds lying idle at the bank, money for which they are constantly seeking investments.

The experiment would, it is true, be a novel one for co-operators, but of late years a marked change has come over the spirit of these great organizations, and we have seen that, so far from resting contentedly on their laurels, they have launched out boldly into housing and other interesting and ambitious schemes. There is already one co-operative quarry, Pantreiniog, and the figures show that, although hampered by lack of capital, it pays. Why should not the great societies of the North, whose members are by no means content that the principles of co-operation should apply only to groceries and the like, who command vast resources, with much business capacity and initiative, why should they not take the matter in hand? At all events, the quarrymen here are resolved to put the matter to the test. It will be most interesting to watch the outcome of the movement – a movement that bids fair to open a new chapter in the emancipation of industry. There is no chance of the landlord squeezing out the profits – a most important consideration. Moel Faban can be leased from the Crown for fifty-nine and a-half years, at a merely nominal rental, in addition to the usual royalty of one-fifteenth of the output. The present owner of the quarry will, of course, have to be settled with, but his terms are not exorbitant. Practically, there is no charge on the land.

That the matter is of incalculable importance to the quarrymen cannot be disputed. The capital that releases the minerals from Moel Faban will set free the men from bondage.

The men are at present absolutely dependent upon Lord Penrhyn's pleasure for the right to live. I can best bring this home to my readers by setting forth, in the actual words of the victim, the feeling of a veteran quarryman discharged from the quarry after a life's devoted service. 'When Mr. Young told us that we were dismissed,' says this veteran, 'we trembled, and our cheeks paled, because we saw no means of gaining our livelihood, and with tears in our eyes we entreated Mr. Young to reconsider his decision. We told him that one of us had worked in the quarry for fifty years, and the other for thirty-five . . . Our appeal was coldly rejected.'

This man was no coward. Without nerve and courage his work could not have been performed. But he knew that when Lord Penrhyn denied him employment he could get it nowhere else. He knew that his wife and children would starve, that he himself would linger on to a useless, miserable old age, without even the pittance that the management dignify with the name of pension. Little wonder that he blanched when the dread sentence of dismissal was read out to him. Little wonder that the quarrymen patiently endure insult upon insult rather than run the risk of being cut off at one blow from all possibility of employment. The cases of arbitrary dismissal from the quarry would fill a volume – a volume that would move all England to pity these veterans of industry sent out at the close of life's battle, broken, condemned to end their days in poverty, often not knowing what offence they had committed!

I call to mind a back page of Penrhynism that is peculiarly interesting in this connection. The last time there was open voting in Carnarvon, the present Lord Penrhyn, then Mr. Pennant, sought the suffrages of the electors for Parliament. He was unsuccessful. Fifteen of his father's employees voted against him. The history of those fifteen men is very instructive. A very few years later every one of them had been discharged from the quarry.

That incident does not stand alone. Mr. W. R. Evans, the Chairman of the Men's Committee during the 1897 strike, was dismissed for a reason that was little better than childish. Others have been dismissed for no reason at all, and, as I have said, once the sentence of ex-communication has been passed upon them, they may abandon hope.

It is clear, therefore, that the possibilities of opening up some new avenue of employment to these victims of Lord Penrhyn's pride has a supreme interest for all who desire to see the quarrymen win their struggle for independence, who will watch the attempt with something more than good will. The present proposal is that a company shall be formed and promoted, much upon the same lines as proved so successful in regard to the Garden City.

The one question that remains, therefore, is that raised by Mr. Henry Vivian, the energetic secretary of the Labour Co-Partnership Association, in his interesting letter to The *Daily News*. 'Does the proposed enterprise,' he asks, 'afford a reasonable hope of meeting expenses and yielding a small profit?' In a word, Will it pay?

That issue, I take it, resolves itself into three considerations, (1) Is there a sufficiency of slate in the mountain? (2) Is that slate of a marketable quality? And (3) can it be cheaply and expeditiously raised to the surface, and put on the market? On the answers to these questions depends the future of the enterprise. I propose, therefore, to deal with them separately.

First, as to quantity. That the mountain is full of slate I have no doubt whatever. The slate rocks crop up under one's feet all over the two hundred and sixty acres comprising the estate. It is found again along the sides of the tunnel, some hundred and twenty yards long, which has been driven in at right angles to the hill; and it is, further, to be seen at the other side of the mountain, being hewn down from the walls of the miniature quarry. So much for the question of quantity. On this head, I call no expert evidence for the moment. But, on the question of the quality of the slate, I proceed to cite one weighty authority, and it will be seen that his statement expressly supports the view that an abundance of slate exists.

Some years ago Mr. John J. Evans, F.R.S., who for a long period was the chief manager of the Penrhyn quarry, and an admitted geological expert, drew up a report on Moel Faban. I have that report before me as I write, and I propose to quote its remarks as to the marketable quality of the slate. They are as follows:

'The colour of the slate is marketable and the cleavage good, and the rock contains plenty of natural joints, which is an important matter in quarry operations.

'The beds of slate which form the surface in this property are (1st) the Green Slate, and (2nd) the Upper Purple Slate of the Cambrian formation, out of which a considerable quantity of marketable slates have been made and are now on the quarry.

'The other beds of slates of the Cambrian formation, which are found in the Penrhyn and other quarries of Carnarvonshire, must be following under these beds in their natural position; but, inasmuch as the angle of the bedding is nearly following the slope of the hill to the north-west, as far as the boundary of the property, the Lower Slate beds are not exposed on the surface within the boundaries of this grant; but to those who are acquainted with the Great Slate formation of Carnarvonshire, to find the upper beds as they are to be found here is sufficient to satisfy them that the lower beds must be following in their natural position and rotation, and that the quantity of slate rock within the property is sufficient to work a quarry of considerable size in it.'

So much for expert evidence. The slate is purple and green, the most marketable colours. The beds are opposite the Penrhyn quarries – the most famous in the world – and according to the best geological opinion obtainable, they are of the same formation. Moreover, there is

– according to this same opinion – slate amply sufficient to work a large quarry.

Mr. Evans does not stand alone in these conclusions. The belief that the Penrhyn vein runs straight through the country from Llanberis, on through and beyond Moel Faban – taking in Pantreiniog on the way – is well-nigh universal in the district, a district, be it noted, which abounds in practical quarry men and geologists. Those who are entitled by years of experience to speak with authority – men who have spent their lives in the district in intimate association with quarry management – have strongly urged this view upon me. And, in addition, I find it supported by a report of Mr. R. H. Parry, of Llanberis, who writes therein that if 'the principal vein (the Penrhyn) . . . comes up to the expectation of all experienced quarrymen that know anything about it, it will be a quarry worth tens of thousands of pounds, and capable of being worked on a scale as extensive as the Penrhyn Quarry.'

But facts are of more importance than opinions, however weighty, and these I have been at pains to obtain. It needs no expert to detect the Penrhyn blue, and the slate now being raised from the quarry is certainly of that colour. The price it commands varies according to the sizes, but it averages about two guineas a ton – a figure that should largely increase as deeper excavations bring larger slates to the surface. Last year, with only two men employed, the profit on slates sold exceeded the outlay by about 40 per cent. That this ratio of profit could be maintained after heavy expenditure on machinery, &c., is not, of course, pretended, but it would be well to recollect in this connection that the green slate commands a very high price in the market, and that the property is capable of producing, not merely roofing slates, but slabs for billiard tables, while the slate debris from the quarry is well adapted for the making of bricks, tiles, and glass.

So much for the quantity and quality of the slate; the question remains, can it be easily 'gotten up' to the surface?

On this point, I again quote from Mr. Evans:

'The position of the property,' he says, 'is such as will afford great facilities for working the quarry in a cheap manner, being situated on the side of a steep hill, where tunnels can be driven at a comparatively small cost for the purposes of draining the quarry and bringing out the materials.'

41

Once on the surface it will not cost very much to get the slate on the market. Moel Faban is within hailing distance of the London and North Western Station at Bethesda. The cost of getting the slate from the mountain to the railway would be trifling did not Lord Penrhyn, here as elsewhere, block the way. The largest quarry proprietor of North Wales well understands the value of the maxim 'Reach forth and corner.' He has very astutely purchased the land round the base of Moel Faban, and accordingly the slates cannot be taken down an inclined tram line, but must be conveyed to the station by carts along the public road, at a cost of about two shillings per ton. Another two shillings will take them to an adjacent seaport (not Bangor, for here, again, Lord Penrhyn forbids), where ample wharfage and accommodation has been provided by the London and North Western Railway Company. There is no insuperable difficulty, therefore, and no great charge involved, in the question of transit, while we have expert opinion that the quarry affords 'great facilities' for cheap working.

Of course, the certainty of profit cannot be finally resolved until it is seen precisely how the quarry develops. At present the aggregate price of the slates raised amounts, as I have said, to two guineas per ton. This figure gives little guidance, however. The more the quarry is developed the larger the slates become, and accordingly the higher the price per ton. But from figures supplied to me from an adjacent quarry, it is estimated that every fifteen 'bargains' (as the pieces of rock let to three quarrymen are called) produce a net profit of about a thousand pounds per annum. This, of course, is only a rough and ready guide so far as Moel Faban is concerned. Let there be no doubt upon one point, however – the matter deserves the closest attention of all who desire to free the quarrymen. The opening of a successful rival quarry to the Penrhyn would spell deliverance to Bethesda. It would mean the salvation of the place. The task of wringing just conditions from Lord Penrhyn is made enormously difficult by reason of the fact that he has a virtual monopoly of all the employment to be offered in the district. He is the one 'master.' Owning the only considerable industry in the neighbourhood, he has a power almost of life and death over nearly every workman. Without Lord Penrhyn's permission they cannot get employment, and that permission is only given them on terms which they find intolerable. Clearly, therefore, if other employment can be offered to the men on a large scale, by the working of other quarries, the best means possible will have been adopted to stay the destruction of this upright and gifted race. 'The one element of hope,' a minister said to me yesterday, 'lies in the development of these quarries.' And, looking at the enormous difficulties that front one on every other side, I am not sure he was not right.*

* Since these words were written two experts have been commissioned to inquire and report on the commercial prospects of Moel Faban. It is also interesting to note that there is some possibility of getting some of the men employed in other quarries, thus further modifying Lord Penrhyn's monopoly.

W. J. Parry (1842-1927), a close friend of Charles Sheridan Jones. He was the first Secretary of the North Wales Quarrymen's Union and he played an active and prominent role in defence of the quarrymen's cause throughout his life. A staunch Liberal and Independent Congregationalist, he published several books and wrote scores of articles for newspapers and periodicals

CHAPTER VIII

THE FUTURE OF THE FIGHT

WHAT are the prospects of the future? It is a baffling question, but one thing is certain – there can be no surrender. Here, on the spot, this comes convincingly home to one. Standing on the top of Llandegai Mountain, looking down on Bethesda, the home of a people, one realises that this is not a mere question of a rise of wages; it is not even only a fight for a principle. What is at stake is the existence of a race, small it may be, but with a distinct personality, if personality means resistance. Consider how these cottages, in their picturesque simplicity, came into being. They were built by the grandfathers of the present quarrymen, who worked with rough tools and bruised hands far into the night to get them erected, and who cemented the bricks literally with their life's blood. And their present occupants cannot bear the thought of surrendering what their forebears made at so terrible a cost. They cling to the old home. Mobility, Labour's chief protection, does not exist for them. It has been the aim of the Penrhyn land policy to tie these people to Bethesda, and that policy has succeeded beyond hope. Even when they seek elsewhere the reasonable conditions denied them here they leave their wives and children at Bethesda, and still keep up the old home.

But sooner than submit to Lord Penrhyn they will abandon even that home. They will leave the mountains and the rivers, and go – who knows where. The race will be destroyed. Their occupation will be gone, their spirit broken. That is the price of surrender, that, and the fact that the men who perforce remain, and go into the quarry, will be embittered and dispirited for life, their morale broken, their faith in man and God destroyed.

What is the chance of this calamity? Those who know the men best declare that never in the whole course of their long struggle have they shown the enthusiasm they now display after a fight, be it noted, of over two years' duration. I will give one instance to support this. I chanced to-day upon Richard Hughes, the fine old Welsh Radical, who, on the present Lord Penrhyn's defeat for Parliament, was, with some eighty other quarrymen, summarily discharged, an injustice which a few years later the much-abused Quarry Committee got remedied. Save for this interval Hughes has worked all his life in the quarry, ever since, in fact, he was a lad of seven. 'For sixty-seven years,' he told me, 'this hand has worked for Lord Penrhyn,' but he had no hope of any pension. His only certain hope, in fact, of ending his last days in comfort is in his immediately re-entering the quarry, and this I pointed out to him. He answered me passionately that he would sooner beg his bread. The answer reflects, I believe, the general spirit which the men are showing.

It is important that this determination of the men to continue the struggle, so long as they are assured of adequate support, should be kept persistently before the public. Startling as it may seem, a rumour has found currency in a section of the Press that the strike is virtually over, and that the continued resistance of a handful of men – so runs the legend – is hopeless. It is time this particular mendacity was nailed down. Newspapers have received it couched in various forms and printed on slips issued nearly every week to the number of some two hundred from an office not a hundred miles away from Penrhyn Castle. The statement is so absurd that one would wonder how it obtained currency or credence, were it not for the fact that it is issued to some dozens of newspapers all over the country nearly every week. I may point out that there are now working in the quarry not more than 920, instead of, as at the beginning of the strike, 2800 men; it is ridiculous to assume on these figures that Lord Penrhyn has conquered. Many of the 'bradyrs' have never before worked in a quarry. Some, whom I have seen, were before the strike hawking fish in Bangor. The fact is that only a small proportion of Lord Penrhyn's former employees have surrendered to him, and that in recruiting from all sorts and conditions of men, and then claiming victory, he is merely playing a characteristic card.

As to the number of men Lord Penrhyn has captured, I have made exhaustive inquiries under this head, and after a close analysis and the careful comparison of many conflicting statements, my view is that Lord Penrhyn has not now more than 900 workmen in regular daily attendance at the quarry. Of these not more than half are skilled quarrymen. Some have never before been inside a quarry. They include small tradesmen, whom the strike has made bankrupt, street hawkers, recruits from the casual wards, young lads and old men, the sweepings, in fact, of the country side. Their latest item is an unemployed barber. We may dismiss as worthless, therefore, the preposterous canard that Lord Penrhyn has already achieved victory; that he has, in fact, no need of the 2000 men who still defy him.

At present those 2000 stand solid. How long will they remain so? The relief now reaching them needs to be enormously increased to meet even Bethesda's barest necessities. And there is one thing even more imperative than increased relief. That is – hope, without which no fight can continue. If, looking ahead, the men still see nothing but weary waiting and privation, then there is danger that Lord Penrhyn may, by the aid of hunger and hardship, recruit by twos and threes till, as the months grow into years, the stalwarts will grow fewer and fewer, their influence diminishing with each secession, till, in unspeakable bitterness of spirit, they shake the dust of the place off their feet for ever.

That in this lies the enemy's hope we have striking proof. To-day his Lordship is building cottages at Tregarth, the 'bradyrs'' retreat. The cottages are let to quarrymen on one condition, that they work in the quarry. And they are let on weekly tenancies. None of Lord Penrhyn's new workmen are to own their houses, or to have leases. They are to be absolutely dependent on favour of the overlord, and revolt in the quarry is to involve a punishment which the Denaby collieries have tasted this week. The fight, in fact, is to go on until a new race of quarrymen, who know Pharaoh too well, have been reared up.

The issue rests with the nation. If it can be brought convincingly home to the quarrymen, that outside Bethesda there exists a vast body of public opinion, which will, at all costs, sustain them in their ordeal, and make it impossible for famine again to menace Bethesda, then the dribble of recruits to Lord Penrhyn's quarry will be dammed. Lord Penrhyn will then see the futility of any hope that the men will be abandoned, and left to his tender mercies. That such a body of opinion exists there can be no doubt whatever. But this body of opinion needs focussing and directing. It has found no adequate expression inside Parliament. I am glad to say there is a movement on foot to end, at least, this unsatisfactory state of things. If Lord Penrhyn is still obdurate, he may expect that his quarries will be frequently heard of at St. Stephen's during the coming Session, and from the platform of the House of Commons the rights and wrongs of the Penrhyn quarrymen will be made clear. If this fine race of men is to be sacrificed on the altar of a nobleman's obstinacy, at least their friends are determined that their wrongs shall be known throughout the nation. And with the nation rests the answer.

THE MORAL OF PENRHYNISM.

THE question raised by Lord Penrhyn is fundamental and far-reaching. It is not merely a question of the right to combine, but of the right to live. The use of land is the first necessity of life and industry. The land is the Nation's home, workshop and storehouse. Those who " own " the land, to them belong the people who cannot live except on and from the land. Lord Penrhyn claims only what all other Land Holders claim. Admit the claim of the Lord of Bethesda to withhold from labour the use of the slate-bearing land, and we admit the right of all other Land Holders to withhold from labour the use of all other lands, be they coal, clay, ironstone, urban or agricultural lands. Hence it is that the real question at issue is of the right of Land Lords to " own," and therefore to control the use of those natural opportunities necessary to the life of all ; and, conversely, of the right of the people to live and labour in " the land which the Lord their God hath given them."

Let the friends of labour see that the Bethesda quarry-men are supplied with funds and saved from starvation; but let them also accept the battle-ground to which Lord Penrhyn so frankly invites them. In the hands of the Nation there is a weapon irresistible and all-powerful : a weapon which would soon bring Lord Penrhyn and all other enemies of labour to their senses. At present it costs Lord Penrhyn nothing to keep his quarries idle. But let all land, all the natural opportunities, *whether in use or withheld from use*, be taxed, say only 5s in the pound of annual value : and, manifestly, Lord Penrhyn's attitude towards his " hands " would soon be a very different one. Thus may the workers easily and speedily enfranchise themselves from the slavery to which their enemies have for centuries combined to condemn them.

Those desirous of promoting this equitable and necessary reform should join—

THE ENGLISH LEAGUE FOR THE TAXATION OF LAND VALUES,
376-377, Strand, London ; or,

THE SCOTTISH SINGLE TAX LEAGUE,
13, Dundas Street, Glasgow.

Minimum subscription, 1s a year.

The monthly paper of the Leagues—*Land Values*—is posted monthly to every Member who pays an Annual Subscription of 2s 6d or more to the funds of either League.

SUBSCRIPTION FORM.

To the Secretary,

London Central Committee, Penrhyn Quarrymen's Relief Fund,

168, Temple Chambers, E.C.

Dear Sir,

I herewith enclose you..................................pounds..................

shillings and................pence, being my subscription to the Penrhyn Quarrymen's Relief

Fund, which please have acknowledged in the " Daily News," London, E.C.

Yours truly,

Signature.....................................

Address....................................

Date....................................

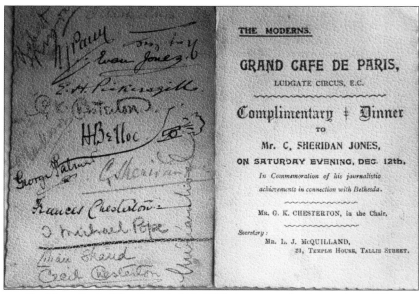

The Menu Card of the dinner held in CSJ's honour, under the auspices of The Moderns, at the Grand Café de Paris, Ludgate Circus, London, 'In Commemoration of his journalistic achievements in connection with Bethesda', with the signatures of some of the guests jotted on the back cover

Charles Sheridan Jones in his late 40s

Charles Sheridan Jones with his family in the garden of The Orchard at Ashdon, Essex, c.1924. With him are his wife, Marion, and his elder daughter Elizabeth, with his other two daughters, Mary and Charlotte, in the front

Mary Barnett, youngest daughter of Charles Sheridan Jones, in 1982. This photgraph was taken in Blaenau Ffestiniog when Mary was attending a course on the Slatemaking Industry of North Wales at nearby Plas Tan-y-Bwlch

Charles Sheridan Jones

APPENDIX

A pamphlet published by the Editor of the *Daily News* in October 1902.

Lord Penrhyn's Methods
The Press Gag, and How it was Burst

Price One Penny

[The proceeds of the sale of this pamphlet will be given to the Bethesda Quarrymen's Fund]

Extract from the Daily News, October 4th

WE have received the following letter from Lord Penrhyn's solicitors:

Re PENRHYN QUARRY STRIKE
BANGOR, NORTH WALES
Sept. 27th, 1902

Sir, – Lord Penrhyn's attention has been drawn to an article on this subject contained in your issue of the 25th inst., headed 'Black Wednesday at Bethesda,' and he has instructed us to write to you thereon.

The article contains a number of absolutely false and libellous statements, and is calculated to prejudice Lord Penrhyn's interest in the action for libel which, as you are no doubt aware, he has commenced against Mr. W. J. Parry, of Bethesda, in which some of the very issues which you falsely represent are involved. Under these circumstances we are instructed to inform you that, if any repetition of the statements complained of, or like statements, appear in any future issue of your paper whilst the matters referred to are sub judice, application will be forthwith made to the Court for your committal for contempt. And we are further instructed to inform you that Lord Penrhyn holds you responsible in damages for the injury which you have or may have inflicted upon him by the article complained of and other articles in your newspaper, and legal proceedings will in due course be taken against you in respect thereof. – We are Sir, your obedient servants,

CARTER, VINCENT & Co.

To the Editor of the *Daily News*.

53

The Gauntlet Picked Up

ONE OF MANY EXTENDED TO THE PRESS

To this threat the journal gave the following crushing reply:

We publish to-day a letter from Lord Penrhyn's solicitors which raises in a most vital form the whole question of the rights of the Press in this country to comment on matters of public moment. The letter contains two threats. The first and less important is a threat of action for libel on the ground of statements made in an article contained in the *Daily News* on September 25th, and written by our Special Correspondent at Bethesda. The nature of that article may be judged from the letter written by the same pen, also from Bethesda, which we publish to-day. Neither of those letters contain anything but an honest description of the facts concerning one of the most important events of the day. If the facts are black, that is Lord Penrhyn's own fault. We do not wonder that this implacable man should dislike our Correspondent's faithful description of the wholesale misery of this unhappy community. But if Lord Penrhyn imagines that he can silence the voice of this journal by such threats as these, he is labouring under a complete delusion. We shall continue, in spite of his threats, to publish such accounts of the long-drawn tragedy which is being enacted in Bethesda as we feel the public ought to have. We shall continue to describe the slow destruction of

An Industrious and God-fearing Community

and to appeal to the Trade Unions of England and Wales not to stand by and watch this struggle without an effort to help the men who are fighting their own cause, but who – as our Correspondent describes to-day – are at the point of starvation for want of funds. We are perfectly content to leave the decision as to these articles to any impartial mind, and Lord Penrhyn may understand once and for all that we are not to be frightened out of our duty to these men, and to the public of this country.

The second threat put forward by Lord Penrhyn's solicitors is of a nature which we should not care to characterise. It seems that Lord Penrhyn has an action hanging over the head of Mr W. J. Parry, of Bethesda, as to the details of which we neither know nor care anything.

But if he imagines that either public opinion or the law of this land will enable him to use it as

An Instrument for Gagging Newspapers

he is vastly mistaken and misinformed. This very point arose in a recent case, in which it was clearly decided that so long as no direct allusion was made to the action or proceedings, there could be no case of contempt. We alluded neither directly nor indirectly to Lord Penrhyn's action. We were not aware of it, nor interested in it. We were dealing simply with a great question affecting not only the fundamental relations of capital and labour, but full of the most poignant human pathos. Lord Penrhyn must study the law of contempt. He may be the

Sole Survivor of Feudal Institutions

but he is not a Judge of the High Court. He may be able to empty a village by his actions, and to scatter a stalwart race, which might form a bulwark to this country in some hour of trouble, to the four winds of heaven. He may even, if English workmen be indifferent, be able to bring these quarrymen to their knees, as braver men have been brought to their knees, by the sufferings of their women and children. But he is not yet above the law, and criticism of his action is not yet subject to summary jurisdiction. If, indeed, Lord Penrhyn proved to have the law behind him in such a threat, we should be faced with an intolerable state of affairs. In any great matter of public moment, criticism could be silenced by the issue of a writ. A libel action brought by Mr Arthur Balfour against Dr Clifford might silence us on the Education Bill. An action by Mr Brodrick against Mr Winston Churchill might debar us from criticising the conduct of the South African war. We are not aware of the points which Lord Penrhyn has raised in his actions against Mr Parry, of Bethesda. The details seem to belong to ancient history. But we are quite sure that our articles have referred only to the matters of public import raised by a labour struggle which has now acquired an

Exceptional and almost National Importance

and Lord Penrhryn may be well assured that no writs brought against any of his local opponents will be considered by us for one moment as a bar to our right of criticism.

It is high time, indeed, that the nation awoke to the terrible wear and waste involved in the prolongation of this struggle in the Bethesda district. It seems now to be an accepted notion in this country that these destructive struggles between Capital and Labour should be allowed to continue without outside interference until one side or the other is worn out. That is not a view which commends itself to President Roosevelt. We describe elsewhere the efforts made by

That Alert and Fine-spirited Ruler

to bring to a close the great labour war which is already depriving the United States of their proper coal supplies. The American coal struggle is a far greater matter than the conflict at Bethesda. It threatens America with a famine of warmth. But it raises precisely the same issue. In the American coal mines, as in the Bethesda quarry, the men have always advocated arbitration, and the employers always refused it. In the American case, as in the Welsh, the fight arises over the refusal of the masters to deal with the men through their elected Union representatives. In other words, in both cases the principle of combination is at issue. In both cases the attempt of the employer is to return to the old individual relationship where the workman is surely driven to the wall by his individual weakness. In both cases the men have made every possible appeal to their employers, and in the Bethesda case those who have followed our Correspondent's letters will have watched day by day the slow death of the last lingering hope for some reasonable compromise. Across the water President Roosevelt recognises these things, and is working, even in illness, to allay this grievous trouble. What public man is doing the same here?

Which of our Ministers is Stirred by the Sufferings of Bethesda?

Which of them knows anything about such things? We have an Arbitration Act, which cannot be applied without the consent of both parties, and a Board of Trade in the possession of a Minister who is a rigid doctrinaire of the old school. We have just heard from Mr Seddon his rosy accounts of compulsory arbitration, but such good news has but stirred us in our sleep. How long are these things to go on? Here is a struggle which has continued for five years with but a short interval of abatement. It has brought grievous suffering. It has scattered a community. Are such matters of no account to our public men that they should pass by on the other side? Surely it is the duty of the great Trade Unions to see that this forlorn hope is not lost – that this outpost is not captured – and to force the rulers of this country to attend to this cry of suffering humanity.

The Penrhyn Lock-out

What is at Stake

AN INTERVIEW WITH THE MEN'S SECRETARY
From the *Daily News.*

Mr Daniel, the Secretary of the Quarrymen's Union in North Wales, is at present in London, and as no one knows more about the circumstances of the labour struggles in the Bethesda quarries during the last ten years, we have asked him to give us a brief statement of the points at issue. This he has kindly done to a representative of the *Daily News.*
    The first question put to Mr Daniel by our representative was as to the primary origin of the Bethesda struggles.

The Quarry Committee

'What,' he asked, 'is this Quarry Committee for which the men are always asking, and which Lord Penrhyn is always refusing?'

> 'To answer that,' said Mr Daniel, 'we must go back nearly thirty years. The Quarry Committee was founded in the seventies. Upon the termination of the fourteen weeks' strike at the Penrhyn Quarries in 1874 an agreement was arrived at, known as the Pennant Lloyd Agreement, by which the men were empowered to form a committee from among themselves to consider grievances, and bring them to the notice of the management. That was the Quarry Committee. Lord Penrhyn abolished it in 1885 – and it is to the restoration of this committee that he is so averse. His great objection to it rests on the

assertion that it controlled and managed the quarry. To show how utterly unfounded such a charge is, it only requires to be pointed out that the referee and arbitrator under that agreement was none other than Lord Penrhyn's own estate agent.'

'Then what possible objection can Lord Penrhyn have to its renewal?'

' "Interference" – he says that it interferes between employer and employed, and he defies us to quote any Act of Parliament which will compel him to recognise it. "You can combine" he says, "if it amuses you, but I decline to recognise your combination in any dealings with you." Here are his words, used during a conference that took place during the last dispute:

> Meanwhile, I can only repeat what I have before said, and what you are perfectly well aware of, that is, that you are entitled to combine in any lawful way, that is to say, in any way sanctioned by Act of Parliament; but I shall continue to contend for the absolute freedom of both employer and employed from any interference or dictation by a committee. If you wish me to add anything to what I have already said, it will be in the form of a query addressed to yourselves, as to where you can find in any Act of Parliament anything which compels an employer of labour to recognise the authority of a committee which seeks to interfere with direct communication between employer and employed. Unless you can show that such an Act of Parliament exists, and that I think you know well enough is not the case, you are seeking to do something which is outside the law when you endeavour to enforce the intervention of such a committee upon your employer.

'It is quite clear,' continued Mr Daniel, 'that combination of this kind would be entirely useless for any purpose whatever.'

The 1897 Agreement

'But,' urged our representative, 'did you not fight this matter out in the strike of 1896-7, and come to a definite agreement?'

'At the end of the 1896-7 strike the men had to accept an agreement which gave them only a limited and restricted right of combination, under which the grievances were to be brought before the management by means of sectional representation. It was the best that we could get at the time, and it might have worked if a good spirit had existed in the dealings of Lord Penrhyn and his workmen. But the agreement never worked satisfactorily.'

Cases of Injustice

'How did it work? Can you give me any instances?'

'One of the first to make use of its provisions was the Chairman of the Strike Committee, Mr W. R. Evans, who had worked for Lord Penrhyn for fifty-two years. Yet when he approached the chief manager under the agreement, was only told that the interview was "granted to him in order to impress on his mind and the mind of others that he, Mr Young, could expel whom he wished without giving his reasons."

'This,' continued Mr Daniel, 'was only one of several cases of harsh and arbitrary conduct on the part of the management. In a word, the agreement was a mockery. We soon found that Lord Penrhyn had not budged an inch from his position. The "sectional" representation was only the latest phrase for individual dealing. Several men who have taken part in these "sectional" deputations have been discharged without adequate reason given. The result has been that the men have been thrown back on themselves, and there has been a constant accumulation of petty personal grievances, producing a bitter feeling against the management. This feeling, combined with the fear that the contract system would be extended, and the harsh discipline enforced, culminated in the unfortunate attack on the contractors.'

The Grievances

'Suppose, Mr Daniel, that the right of combination were awarded, what are the grievances that the men wish to press on the management?'

'I may sum them up as follows:

1. They desire the reinstatement of certain victimised men. This point Lord Penrhyn has refused to discuss.
2. They desire the free use of the dinner-hour in the quarry. At present the men are prevented from holding meetings in any part of the

quarry, or from collecting any subscriptions. Now, the quarry is virtually their collective living place; for the men's homes are scattered over a large area, and it is almost impossible for them to meet at any other place or time. They all carry their food, as it is impossible for them to get out of the quarry for dinner, owing to its great size. They have, therefore, a considerable time to spare during the dinner-hour, and it seems a peculiarly unnecessary hardship that they should be forbidden to meet and discuss their interests.

3. They desire a minimum wage of 4s. 4d. a day.

4. They desire the abolition of the contract system, but are willing to test the point by experiment. They object to the bullying of the contractors and subordinate officials, and wish to deal direct with the management.

5. They consider that the rules of discipline are too harsh (a man who is 15 minutes late loses half-a-day's pay – over 15 minutes a whole day).

6. They desire more democratic management of the Benefit Club.

7. They wish for the right of an annual holiday.

These grievances were discussed between Mr Young and four representatives on Dec. 19th, 1900. He refused any concession either on the right of combination or on the first three points. With respect to the contracting system, he suggested the experiment of co-operative contracts in a part of the quarry where contracts did not at present exist. This the men naturally regarded as a simple extension of the contract system. On the remaining points he was more conciliatory; but you will see that he refused any substantial concession, and on the proposals being submitted to the men they were rejected by 1,707 votes to 77.'

How Long? How Long?

'You speak of December, 1900. Since when has the present struggle been going on?'

'It began on Nov. 22nd, 1900; but owing to the suspension of the men before the strike as a punishment for the attack on the contractors, they have really been out of the quarry for two years. Negotiations broke off because Lord Penrhyn refused to discuss any modification in the 1897 agreement. Remember that the men are not asking for the recognition of their Union officials, but for the barest rights of combination, in the recognition of their Quarry Committee. Perhaps I cannot do better than quote the men's own appeal to the Trade Unions in February, 1901:

> After the last great fight the Manager victimised the men's leaders, and the fight is now for 'to establish our right' to appear before the management by our own freely elected delegates. We have not gone so far even as to ask for the recognition of our Union. We merely ask to freely elect spokesmen from our own ranks in the quarry, for the purpose of discussing grievances from time to time with the management. We are denied this right; we are denied the right to discuss grievances in the quarry among ourselves in our own time during the dinner-hour. We are not treated as men. We are sworn at, abused, and libelled. We are subject to a system of espionage. We are punished for fictitious offences; if a few minutes late we were suspended for two days. One of our customary holidays has been taken from us, and many of our number are compelled to work under the sweating system, without any real chance of redressing grievances when they arise. The management is harsh and oppressive in spirit, and failing to understand the men, it results in friction and grievances, which, without any means of amelioration, become intolerable to men who respect their manhood.

How Many?

'We are now clear as to the issue. Could you tell me precisely the number of men involved; how many men are now out, and how many in?'

> 'The full quota of the men employed at the quarries before the dispute was 2,800. A small section of men seceded in June, 1901, and there are now employed in the quarries from 700 to 800. Not half of these are quarrymen, even if we include all officials and boys. Over 2,000 are still outside the quarry. Of these, some 1,200 are working, either in South Wales or elsewhere, leaving some 800 to be provided for by the Union funds, besides all the people who are involved in the distress, and are looked after by the Relief Committee.'

Arbitration Accepted

'You do not refuse arbitration, or feel any unwillingness to submit to the Conciliation Act?'

'On the contrary, we have always been willing to submit our case to arbitration, and would accept with joy such a Commission as has been appointed by President Roosevelt to settle the American coal strike. If the Board of Trade sent down a Commissioner to report under the Conciliation Act, we would give him every facility and assistance. We are content that our case should be submitted to the judgment of any impartial men, because we are convinced of the justice of our cause. Meanwhile, we appeal to the whole country to help us in our struggle.'

Starving Bethesda!

A Letter from the *Daily News* Special Correspondent

TO-DAY should be a proud one for the subscribers to the *Daily News* Fund for the quarrymen. This morning's meeting of the Relief Committee marked a triumph for their efforts. The meeting was their triumph, first of all, because, as the Chairman pointed out, but for the *Daily News* there would have been no meeting at all, or at best only an abortive one. It was a triumph, again, because the Committee, greatly daring, virtually decided to organize distributions twice, and not, as formerly, once a month; but chiefly it was a triumph because of the decision to grant relief in certain cases to the families of unemployed strikers now receiving the Trade Union allowance – a much needed protection for that hard-pressed flank of the men's army, the seven hundred strikers now at Bethesda. In all there were 725 cases reported to the Committee as requiring instant relief, and as no less than 130 of these came from Caellwyngrydd, I decided to spend the day in that district, two members of the Committee kindly volunteering to show me round.

Starving Caellwyngrydd

Caellwyngrydd has for months past been a starving district. I question if anywhere else in the world can there be found a parallel for the spectacle it presents – that of a number of skilled workmen, temperate and thrifty to a degree, yet lacking with their wives and children the actual necessaries of life. It is impossible for me to describe the scenes that I witnessed to-day in the homes of these half distracted people, and fortunately I need not do so. The facts are eloquent, and speak for themselves. I need only set out in skeleton form some of the more representative cases which I have selected from a mass of others.

Take first the case of Mrs Richard Jones. Her house was, I found, absolutely bare though scrupulously clean. When I and the Committeemen arrived she was cutting some bread that she herself had made into slices. That bread was the only food she had in the house with which to stay her five children's hunger, and but for the Relief Committee (who had supplied the flour) she would have lacked even that. She had not a drop of milk. She was without so much as a lump of sugar. There was a little burnt treacle and some tea leaves, that had been used over and over again. This was all she could add to the brew to make the children's meal. It is small wonder that they looked haggard and worn. They had known worse times: their mother told me that once, half demented, she had gone out and begged from door to door for food. She had to walk far before she could find anyone to give her more than pity. In this case the husband, a striker, has been unemployed for eighteen months. At the commencement of the present struggle he got work in the Lancashire Collieries, but an accident compelled him to return home. He and his family have had nothing since to live upon except the Union allowance of 10s. a week. Now, thanks again to the *Daily News*, the Relief Committee will be able to add at least a trifle to this wretched sum.

Suffering and Misery

I found an even sadder case. At the next cottage we visited we were faced by a woman in the last extreme of suffering and misery. She herself was expecting very shortly to be confined. Her husband lay prostrate with rheumatism. She had literally nothing in the house with which to get food, and her husband's strike allowance of ten shillings a week from the Quarrymen's Union did not become due till next month. True, the husband has been unemployed only for a week or two, but his earnings (he worked at Rhayadr) have not admitted of his sending more than ten shillings a week home, and his wife has nothing to fall back upon now that she is ill, and her two children are clamouring for food. Small wonder therefore that she burst into tears when told that a grant had been made her from the Relief Committee. That grant, alas, was only six shillings, but to her it was priceless. Her children would be fed at last. My own feelings I do not chronicle. Indeed, if I allowed my mind to dwell upon the facts I could not state them at all. One marvels as one visits cottage after cottage in this stricken district at the extraordinary dogged honesty of the people. Nearly all of them told me with a touch of pride that they had paid their rent – a matter of two shillings to half a crown a week – all through this dreadful time. Among all these sufferers I did not find one single waverer. The men all scouted the idea of returning to the quarry on Lord Penrhyn's 'terms' of unconditional surrender. The women answered even more fiercely. 'I would sooner die,' one told me, 'rather than that he should go in.'

On the hillside leading up to Moel Faban (where are the unworked quarries referred to in your issue of to-day) we met two women wretchedly clad. One was looking after some sheep; the other, Mrs Morgan, the wife of an unemployed striker, has two children, and nothing but the strike allowance. Her children were fed practically on the potatoes that she raised in her garden. Another woman told me that she had supported herself for months by gathering cockles; and more than one confessed that but for the Relief Committee and occasional credit from tradespeople they must have succumbed.

Need of Further Help

The *Daily News* has removed that danger, but the suffering that still remains is terrible. Consider the case of Albert Rutglede. Before the strike he was gardener to a quarry official. His wife's brothers were strikers, and the official urged Rutglede to get them to submit, but the gardener preferred to stick to his work and was accordingly discharged. To-day I found his wife in tears, sobbing her heart out over a child. Her husband does odd jobs in the district, and manages to bring home perhaps seven shillings a week. Frequently she told us she has been for a fortnight without coal. She has to pay six shillings a month for rent, and can barely keep body and soul together. Her house was the model of cleanliness. It is by struggles such as these that the men and women of Bethesda maintain the struggle. That they cannot do so without further aid is obvious. Famine for the moment is staved off; but if help slackens, nay, if it doesn't instantly increase, its menace will be instantly renewed. The men have shown unexampled fortitude, marvellous endurance. Only three of their number have given in to Lord Penrhyn since this nobleman's trump card, the rupture of the negotiations, was thrown down. It will be a thousand pities if their heroic fortitude goes for nothing.

Freedom or Slavery?

Let there be no doubt as to the issue at stake. The whole history of the Penrhyn struggle shows it to be between freedom and slavery. There can be no doubt whatever that if Lord Penrhyn triumphs the men's morale will be utterly shattered and broken. They will in very truth be helots. I doubt if even yet the public realise the full significance of the regime at the quarries; bad as it is to-day, it would be infinitely worse were Lord Penrhyn's power unchecked. I can prove this by a reference to the past. In 1884, when the men were weak, a deputation from them waited on the present Lord Penrhyn, then the Hon. George Sholto Douglas Pennant. That high-minded and chivalrous aristocrat heard their leaders' statements, and then, calling the three Unionist members of the deputation before him, he read out to them a peremptory notice of dismissal. These men had worked in the quarry all their lives, and not a single complaint had ever been made against their work or their character. Two of them had been in the quarry for over thirty years. So great was the indignation roused among the men by this savage act, that they threatened to strike if their leaders were not reinstated. Nominally this was done, but the Unionists were marked men. They were told that the managers would be specially desired to report on their future conduct.

'Divine Right of the Landlord'

Lord Penrhyn has not deigned to even acknowledge the last letter which the men's leaders sent him. The fact is, that Lord Penrhyn presents grossly and palpably the old feudal view – the Divine right of the landlord to do what he likes with his own. The men who are suffering to-day urge that it is their skill and toil which give value to the quarry, and surely they have some claim to control the conditions of their own labour. It is, in fact, a natural fight between the old idea and the new – a perfectly typical phase of the great world conflict of our time. That the sufferers are not to be deserted in this hour of bitter trial the *Daily News* has made clear, but the need of 'support' is vital still, as all who have seen this stricken division of the army of labour will agree.

One word I should say in conclusion as to the disused quarries in this district, referred to by another correspondent in your issue of to-day. I have been carefully sifting the evidence as to their possibilities. Though there are difficulties in the way of a decision, yet there seems good ground, as I hope to show shortly, for the expectation that with sufficient capital to develop them the blight of Penrhynism might be done away with for ever.

PENRHYN QUARRYMEN'S LOCK-OUT

LONDON CENTRAL RELIEF FUND COMMITTEE
Chairman – E. H. PICKERSGILL.
Treasurer – JOHN KEALEY.
Secretary – C. SHERIDAN JONES.
Offices-168, TEMPLE CHAMBERS, TEMPLE AVENUE, E.C.

The Committee EARNESTLY APPEAL for SUBSCRIPTIONS in support of the locked-out Penrhyn Quarrymen and their families.

The Members of Trade Unions and Clubs, of Friendly and Co-operative Societies, Ministers of Religion, and Individual Sympathisers are specially invited to further the Committee's efforts to obtain funds.

To that end, regular Collections could be made at Meetings, Services, Entertainments, and in Workshops. The formation of Local Committees would greatly assist the work.

Sheets, Boxes, and Bottles for collecting, 1d. Tickets to sell, Literature, Speakers, and every Information, supplied by the Secretary of the Committee. Intending helpers should please communicate with him at once.

All remittances should be made payable to Mr. John Kealey, *Daily News*, Bouverie Street, London, E.C. They will be acknowledged in next day's issue of the *Daily News*.